Living the Life of Riley

Catherine Haysome

America Star Books
Baltimore

First printing

Softcover 978-1-63084-134-8
PUBLISHED BY AMERICA STAR BOOKS, LLLP
www.americastarbooks.com

Printed in the United States of America

INTRODUCTION

My name is Catherine Elizabeth Haysome. I am married to Kevin Haysome. This is my second marriage. My first marriage was not a happy one for reasons I do not need to go into at this point. I have 3 children. Michelle, Jonathan and Michael. Their childhoods were not particularly happy ones, but I did my best. I did the very best that I could. All three children are damaged in some way as are most children. I realise that Michelle carries with her major scars and trauma that to this day she cannot face. Her father carries the burden of blame for this and one day I pray she can come to terms with this and speak openly.

My husband Kevin Haysome is one of the kindest, honest people you could ever meet. I was lucky enough to meet Kevin on Saint Patrick's Day in the year 2,000.

This book isn't about the slashed tyres, the white gloss paint thrown over his car or even the threats made to him although you will read about threats made to Kevin by my eldest son Jonathan.

When I met Kevin, Michelle was 18, Jonathan was 16 and Michael was 11. Kevin has never attempted to take the father role with the children although he is a brilliant grandfather to Michelle's children.

Myself and Kevin did not have any children of our own and never ever contemplated having a dog until one day we adopted a 13 year old Yorkshire terrier named Mickie. Mickie, even though he was a little old man introduced Kevin to the joys of dog ownership and the love that can be given unconditionally. Mickie came to us after his owner had passed away and we loved this pooch until he passed away at the age of 15.

We were then introduced to Troy. A 4 month old boxer puppy that didn't seem to understand that he was meant to stop growing. Troy came to with the name firstly of Tyson and then Skye. These came from his breeder and his first owner. Neither name seemed to suit him and so came the name Troy. If you look into the word DESTROYER you will find Troy. We were to learn this and soon.

I am telling this story largely through the eyes of Troy. It is mainly tales of his life and times but now and again I will give you an insight into our lives and what we go through. Some of it is happy, some of it is hilarious. Some of it is extremely sad. Most of all it is from the heart and true.

I am dedicating this book to my husband Kevin John Haysome. Without Kevin I would not be here today.

Thank you for everything you have done for me, what you are doing and for what you will do for me in the future.

All of my love
Forever and always

Catherine

My name is Troy. I am a 6 year old white male boxer. I am quite a large boy, and weigh around seven and a half stone. (45kg) I am not fat though, I am solid muscle. Mummy Cathy says I have love handles around my hips when I sit down. Also mummy Cathy laughs at my back feet. The skin rolls down by my ankles looking like a pair of fallen down socks. It's rude to laugh mummy Cathy. You are no Twiggy yourself. When I was born I lived with my birth mummy with my brothers and sisters. We were all sent when we were about 8 weeks old to live with new mummies in new families. Even then I was quite a chunky boy. Everybody knew I was never going to be small. I was 3 months old and my new parents didn't want me. How could they not want me? I was gorgeous. I was pure white all over except for what looked like eyeliner under one eye. I have also got the blackest eyes you have ever seen.

Soooooo cute!!!. I was taken back to my birth mother. I wasn't wanted. Because I am a white boxer I am deemed worthless. What a cheek. Mummy Cathy and daddy Kevin had just lost their little dog Mickey. They were grieving and not looking for another dog. A friend of daddy Kevin's had a white boxer and both mummy Cathy and daddy Kevin had both said they would maybe like one in the future. Mummy Cathy happened to hear my sad story from a lady called Sue Brown. This was a lady mummy Cathy used to work with. It was arranged for me to come to meet my new parents. I was soooo nervous. Would they like me, would they want me? I bounded around their garden, all legs and ears flying everywhere. Daddy Kevin couldn't believe the size of me for a puppy. I was staying, they loved me. I would never replace Mickey but I now had new parents. I didn't know it then but I was about to become the luckiest dog ever. No-one could ever love me more than my new mummy and daddy. Meet mummy Cathy and daddy Kevin. Daddy Kevin works really hard. He works as a machine operative, welding car parts for a large car company. His hobbies are obviously me, swimming (getting wet), going to see Gym (he is mysterious), playing with a pool (not swimming) and a stick, walking with sticks and following a ball (Golf). Daddy Kevin has a lot of hobbies. He also watches a lot of sport on a big black rectangle on the wall. Football, rugby, golf, anything really!!! Mummy Cathy works in an office. She is a debt collector. Mummy Cathy says she loves her job and the people she works with are fun. Her hobbies are again obviously me and anything to do with me. She also enjoys cooking and using daddy Kevin as a guinea pig to try new recipes. She doesn't really have many hobbies as she is also kept busy with house work. Mummy Cathy says she doesn't have time to go gallivanting around like daddy Kevin. I also have a big sister named Michelle. She spoils me also. Michelle gets me a massive bag of bones from her local butcher. MMMMM, thank you Michelle. She doesn't live very far from us so I get to walk to her house sometimes. Michelle works hard, she cares for the elderly. Michelle has a partner called Alan. He is a very quiet person and I think very shy. He is a fantastic dad to their children. Alan also grows a lot of vegetables in their garden. Now there are four gorgeous children, my nieces and nephew. Lauren who is 13. Lauren lives with her dad at the moment. She is just going through her troubled teens. She is a lucky girl to have 2 families that love her. Michelle misses her a great deal as do her siblings. Next is Shannon. Shannon who is gorgeous 11 years old. She is getting ready to go to senior high school in September. Soooo grown up. She is a really good swimmer and not afraid to try different strokes. Daddy Kevin taught her how to do the butterfly stroke. Now onto Joseph. He is a proper rough and tumble boy. He has a really cheeky face. He is really good at athletics. Maybe an Olympian in the future. He used to be really afraid of me because he had previously experienced nasty dogs. Not nice friendly dogs like me. We are cool together now. Last but not least is Eleanor. What can I say about this little madam? I have never known anything with as much energy as Eleanor. Also she eats more than I do. That is saying something. She is as bright as a button and afraid of nothing. There is also a rabbit that lives in the garden. He doesn't talk; he just stares and twitches his nose. I bet he would taste nice with gravy, yummy. I must remember to ask Michelle.

Well I have to mention grrrr a kitty cat called Penny. Grrrr. She is cute and pretty enough but she is still a cat. Grrrrr. Cats are the enemy. I do not know why they are the enemy but they are. This is my sister's family. Next is my brother Jonathan. He lives with his girlfriend Sarah. They have a little boy who is almost 2 called Dylan. He is a little cutie. Jonathan also has a little girl called Isabella. She is 3 now and lives with her mum Kayleigh. We haven't seen Isabella since she was a baby. Jonathan fell out with Kayleigh and he has moved on with his new family now. Isabella if you read this in the future we all love you. Sarah is now having a little girl also. Mummy Cathy and daddy Kevin do not see Jonathan and Sarah. I know they miss seeing Dylan growing up. Jonathan was mean to both mummy Cathy and daddy Kevin so for now they are apart. I think it is probably for the best. My other brother is Michael. He also doesn't live with me. He has a flat in town and takes care of himself. He gets drunk a lot so is better living on his own. Michael visits lots and has Sunday dinners with us. This always means less for me as he always has seconds. Piggy Michael. Well that is the family and how I came to live with them. I will carry on with my daily stories of life in the Haysome house hold. If I find out who Gym is I will let you know or if you know him pleeeeeease tell me!!!!!!!What a strange day it has been. Mummy Cathy had to get up early to go to work. I was too sleepy to say bye to her. I had just woken up when she came home. I am not a morning person (dog). Mummy Cathy hasn't stopped since she came in. She has washed and dried and put away all washing. Cleaned the house from top to bottom. She also scrubbed the rug. She struggled with that because it is so big and heavy. You are probably not meant to scrub it with washing powder and a scrubbing brush but it looks as good as new now. It is over the swing seat drying. It will probably be there for a week. LOL. Mummy Cathy gave me a piggy leg for being a good boy. You should have seen the mess I made with it. Sorreeee mummy Cathy, but you did give it to me. Mummy Cathy is hoping for a sunny day tomorrow so that she can sit in the garden and enjoy it. Daddy Kevin sent some photo's of his golf place. It is just grass and nothing else. No other dogs or people or nothing. What would I do there? The grass looked very green though. It wouldn't look like that after I had peed on it and run across a few times. It must be really boring watching a little ball rolling on grass. Maybe if I was there I could fetch the ball and take it back to daddy Kevin. He wouldn't have to follow it then. The only problem with this would be, I am not very good at returning things. I could learn though. I am tired now though, it's watching mummy Cathy rushing around today. Yawn..........

Mummy Cathy and daddy Kevin went out really early this morning. (10.45). They have been back half an hour. Mummy Cathy is that lovely brown colour, remember the colour she wouldn't let me be.... , daddy Kevin is an interesting shade of pinkish/red. Apparently mummy Cathy has been a real lazy cow. She has sat/led on beach all day and done nothing. Daddy Kevin said she needed this as she had been poorly. She has had an ice-cream, but not shared. Mummy Cathy said they had been watching other doggies playing on the beach and wished I was better behaved. Oh god, here it comes. Mummy Cathy has got it into head that daddy Kevin is too soft with me. She is going to start training me. When she tells me off at home I listen and do as she tells me so hey who knows. We will have to wait and see. Mummy Cathy wants to be able to take me out and let me off my lead like other doggies do. If she fails I will let you know. As I have said before, I am not naughty I am just over excitable. Mummy Cathy has found a field with a fence all the way round so we are going there tomorrow. Wish me luck!!!! This is soooo funny, daddy Kevin has come home with birdie poo on his t-shirt. Mummy Cathy was giggling about it until daddy Kevin reminded her she had it down her back also!!!! Looks like I is the only one laughing now. Ha-ha. Mummy Cathy is hoping to go out with my sis tomorrow. She always comes home smiling after they have been together. Mummy Cathy has brought some really nice plastic glasses home with her today. I don't she bought them though. Odd. She says will be really handy for clumsy people (grampy Dennis) in the garden. Right then I have been told; even though it is a bank holiday tomorrow I have to go to sleep now. I think this is because training day starts tomorrow. Mummy Cathy is already getting into sergeant major mode.

A massive thank you tonight to my mummy Cathy and daddy Kevin. (Mostly mummy Cathy). They took me to a park and I was allowed off my lead. This is the 1st time I have been trusted since I was a naughty puppy. There were some teenagers playing football and daddy Kevin didn't want to go into the park with me. Good job mummy Cathy had my lead. She marched me straight in and took off my lead. Daddy Kevin gasted his flabber and stood there as I bolted towards the ball. Mummy Cathy stood firm and shouted TROY, NO. I stopped, turned and ran the other way and then back to mummy Cathy. It was fantastic. I had so much freedom. If only I had realised what I had missed out on. I even ignored another dog that was in there. How good am I? When it was time to go, mummy Cathy told me to sit and put my lead back on. I was so good I did as I was told. Mummy Cathy then took it back off because daddy Kevin said I only sat down because I was tired. She gave daddy Kevin the lead and she told me to sit. I sat. Mummy Cathy told daddy Kevin to tell me to stay. He told me to stay and as he walked towards me, I ran like the wind, grinning as I went. Mummy Cathy was laughing and called me back. She told me to sit and stay and put my lead back on me. We then walked back to the car. I was so tired, still am. I went home and had a nap before my chicken dinner. I am now going back to sleep as I have exhaustion. I might not be able to work tomorrow because I am soooo tired. Mummy Cathy says we are going to do this at least 4 times a week. I shall be skinny like a whippet in 2 weeks.

Any way, night night. I shall dream of Freedom.......X

Well what a couple of days I have had. I didn't go onto face book yesterday as when mummy Cathy came home from work she went straight to bed. She was poorly still with her cough. So any way, daddy Kevin came home from work and took me to the park. Mummy Cathy had been nagging him by email when she was working. She says now I am a good boy daddy Kevin needs to man up and take charge of me. He took me to the park by where my brother Jon lives. We didn't see him. Good job because he was mean to mummy Cathy last week and upset her. Grrr. Anyway at the park he took my lead off me and off I went running round as free as a bird. It's lovely to feel the wind in my fur. A man came along with a husky type dog. I was so scared. I acts all big and tough but I am just a big quivering jelly. Daddy Kevin stood by me and held me. The other dog came and sniffed me and kept pushing me with his paws. Well that was it I ran off to hide. He chased me and before I knew it I was having fun and had made a new friend. Daddy Kevin stood chatting to the other doggy's daddy talking and me and husky played. Such fun. Well today not so much fun. I had to go to the vets. I expected to see my Paul; nope I had a new vet. Mummy Cathy did tell me there was no Paul, but I didn't believe her. How could Paul leave and not want to see me. So I was stuck with Emma. She was alright. She weighed me. I was 43 kilo's. She was happy, she said I had lost weight. I didn't tell her I had been on a hunger strike a few weeks ago. That would explain the weight loss. She pulled my hips and legs in all directions and said they were ok. She then pulled my ears about and looked at my teeth, she said I have lovely shiny teeth. She gave me an injection in my bum and squirted some stuff up my nose. Emma said I was lovely. I think she wanted to be my girlfriend but I acted all cool. We will see what happens the next time I see her......After this we went to the park again. I was off my lead again. I am loving this trust thing that is going on. Bloody tiring though all this running around. I had 3 pooh's in park. Every time daddy Kevin picked it up I went again. Soooo funny. Daddy Kevin went to the pool last night. Remember, the pool with a big stick and no towel. He has gone again tonight. He will be as fit as me with all this swimming. I still do not understand what the stick is for. Where's his towel. Daddy Kevin will catch a cold. I am going to sleep now as my legs is aching and I am yawning. Laters...........

I am tired today. All of this going to school and having lessons is tiring. I had to go again today with daddy Kevin. It was raining again. No coat. Daddy Kevin had his coat on. It not matter about poor little me. Daddy Kevin isn't brave like mummy Cathy. He took me to a babies park. SHHHHHH I am not meant to go in the babies park. Daddy Kevin takes me there because it is enclosed. Any babies reading this, I never pee's or pooh's in there. I have nearly cut my feet on the beer cans mind you. What you babies doing drinking in the park I do not know. Haven't you got cots at home to drink in? We didn't stay too long because it was wet and well daddy Kevin had to get home because mummy Cathy had told him to turn the oven on. Daddy Kevin mind you is a proper naughty person. Mummy Cathy has hardly seen him this week. He has gone swimming with his stick on Tuesday night, Wednesday night and again tonight. He isn't even giving his stick chance to dry out!!! Last night he stayed up really late watching telly. Kept me awake because he was munching. I couldn't sleep with the chance of some cheesy balls going begging. Today as he didn't have to go to work he didn't get up until after 1pm. Lazy or what. I tried to wake him up earlier but no luck. Daddy Kevin is going for a long walk with his dad (Grampy Dennis) tomorrow. In between walking they hit little white balls about using funny stick things. Daddy Kevin seems to like stick games. This game isn't in a pool though it is on grass. I would like to have a go but daddy Kevin says I am not allowed. I think he is worried I might beat him. Daddy Kevin and grampy Dennis quite often loose balls. I think this is because when they are walking and talking they forget what they are doing. Apparently, they have to chase the little white ball down a hole. Daddy Kevin takes a lot of different sticks with him in a massive bag. It seems daft taking all that heavy stuff with you on a walk!!!! Men, they are strange. I had an accident earlier. No not that kind of accident. When mummy Cathy came home from work, I was so excited. I took yellow baby to meet her and ran into the garden and dropped him. I came in and had a big cuddle and forgot about yellow baby. He is soaking wet now from being out in the rain and mummy Cathy has pegged him on the washing line. Does this make me a bad parent? Never mind, I still have pink and black baby to sleep with and cuddle. Night night......

Hey, Guess what? I have had a day off doggy lessons today. Because daddy Kevin didn't get back from his gallivanting until gone 7pm, I was too tired to be learning anything. It would have gone straight over mind head at this time of day. It was nearly my bed time really. Daddy Kevin says even athletes get a day off from their training. So today has been a rest day for me. Good news though in case people was worried. Yellow Baby is safe and sound. When mummy Cathy came in from work I had to make do with pink baby. Before she had even hung her bag up she opened the back door and fetched yellow baby from the washing line. OOOh I will sleep better tonight now. My sis Michelle and her family went to a play farm today. I hope they didn't get to muddy playing with the animals. Hang on it might not have been an animal farm, it might have been a growing farm like where Eleanor went with her school. She is so clever, she made pasta at the farm to take home. Michelle said she cooked it and had it for her tea. Yummy. Anyway, back to play farm. Mummy Cathy has just told me it is not a farm at all. I am really confused now. She says it is a safe place for children to go and play in. I wonder if my sis would take me next time. I am only 6. I promise to be gooooooood!!!! Daddy Kevin has had a fun afternoon following a white ball around field. He has red arms to match his red arms. Shhhhhh, don't tell him I have said this. Grampy Dennis is a bit poorly at the moment so it is nice for daddy Kevin to spend time with him on their own. Nanny Brenda and grampy Dennis are going off on a big boat next week to somewhere where it is hot for more than 48 hours. I really hope they have a good time. Sorreeeee nanny Brenda for peeing on your flowers. Oooooh 2 days off work now. No beds and sofas to test. I can just relax on them now. Time for dreams now. Sleep tight.........

Hi everyone, even if I do say so myself I am a very handsome chap. I lead a very exciting life which I will give you all details of in the future as it happens. I live with my adoptive parents, Mummy Cathy and Daddy Kevin. I have 2 brothers and a sister. Jon, Mike and Michelle. I am their brother from another mother. I also have nieces and nephews. Oh such fun to be had with children. They are always eating. MMMMMMM Yummy. I enjoy playing games. One of them is a game Mummy Cathy calls the in out game. I bark to go pee pee. I come in munch on some grub and bark to go out again. I can keep this going for half an hour. Mummy Cathy tries to act cross with me but hey I always get a bikky. I am feeling sleepy now, so see ya later. Only a quick nap cos I can smell dinner and have to guard the oven door. A very important job!!!!!

I am so not wagging my tail. As I said I was having forty winks, only to be interrupted by Mummy Cathy opening the fridge door. Now I have built in sonar for food related noises and smells. There she was making Daddy Kevin's sandwiches for work. Not a crumb or a crust for me. To make matters worse she then opened the oven door to check on roast potatoes. My ribs are seriously sticking out now. If you don't hear from me again you will know I have wasted away!!!! And to cap it all it's raining. Who wants to pee in the rain!!!

Well I don't know what to say. Mummy Cathy and Daddy Kevin have just eaten their dinner. I sat there throughout, I dribbled, I whimpered, and gave my best soppy look and do you know what I got. Well I will tell you. A tiny piece of pastry. Mummy Cathy has put some dog food in my dish and is expecting me to eat it. I might go on hunger strike if I can find the will power. I will let you know how that goes. I am feeling light headed already. Where's my mate Joe with the Jaffa cakes when I need him!!!!!!

I didn't last long with hunger strike. I was fading fast. I felt I was so skinny; there would be an appeal on the telly to feed me. Any way I have eaten my food and am now watching the football with my daddy Kevin. Daddy Kevin has just been finishing his decorating (whatever that means) in the bathroom. I will sate nite nite now as I have had a busy day and I will probably be asleep very soon. I will chat again tomorrow. X

Good Morning all. I not sleep too good last night. Daddy Kevin dragged me out for a long long walk and OMG my legs ached. I couldn't get comfy on any of my beds. I even went upstairs to try my luck on the big bed. No luck yet. I will keep trying!!!! I did sleep on my union jack bed, which Mummy Cathy dragged inside their bedroom so that I wouldn't be lonely. Once I knew I had disturbed her I went back downstairs to the comfy sofas. Who wants to sleep on a dog bed on the floor!!!! Anyways I have been up about for a little while. Time to start work and testing those sofas. It sure is a DOGS life!

Whoops. Mummy Cathy has just got in from work. I was doing my sofa/bed testing so well. I must have dropped off to sleep for a minute because I didn't hear her come in. I think I may have been rumbled. Do you think she has guessed I sleep most of the day away? I am now led on the rug, keeping a low profile. She did just say, my brother Mike is popping round later. I guess he will want feeding. He is mean to me most of the time, he never shares his dinner with me. Oh unless its sprouts, which we both hate. I think they are all having chicken for tea. Yummy. I do love chicken. mmmmmm. I am now busy doing my floor exercises, rolling and spinning around the floor. That's enough of that, I'll give myself a heart attack. Remember I am still weakened from last night's hunger strike. Rest time. Anyway back to my brother Mike. He works in a shop. Whatever that is. He never brings me anything from this shop so it can't be a good shop. Daddy Kevin makes bits for cars. Now cars are sometimes good and sometimes bad. I like going to Nan and gramps house. It takes months and years to get there. (Half hour). Seems like a long time to me! They have a big garden too run around on. They are kind to me. They sometimes get me massive bones to munch on. Not allowed to eat them in the lounge though. I get told I am messy. I really am not, honestly. The bad thing about cars is, they sometimes take me to kennels. Kennels is a place Daddy Kevin and Mummy Cathy take me to. They leave me there for about 3 years. (2 weeks). When they come back they are a different colour. They joke and call it fat camp. They think they are sooo funny. Not. It is like Tenko for dogs. I am traumatised by it forever now. I may have to have therapy. Just thinking about it has brought back the lovely, oh I mean bad memories. Anyways I is off for pee now, catch you all later.

Just a quickie this time. I got side tracked about my Daddy Kevin. Yes he makes bits for cars, but what I was going to say is food connected. Like I said My Michael doesn't share or bring me anything. Well Daddy Kevin is just the opposite. As soon as he gets in from work, I push past him wagging my little tail. Just enough to say I am happy you home. As soon as he puts his work bag down I am on it like a rabbit up a drain pipe. Is that a real saying? Whatever. Getting side tracked again. He nearly always leaves something from his lunch for me. If there is foil or a plastic box I know its treat time. The best bit is, if he hasn't left me something I have worked out a look that makes him feel guilty so that I get a treat of some kind anyway. My favourite is cheese. Mmmmm must have been a mouse in a previous life. Later's

OMG. I cannot believe Daddy Kevin dragged me out in this arctic weather for a walk. Because I am only a small dog (due to the hunger strike mentioned previously), well I could hardly keep four paws on the pavement. My ears were flaying about in the wind, the lashing rain was hitting my face. Worst of all there were two halves of chicken in a barbecue sauce in the oven cooking. What if I had gotten back and they had gone? If that Michael had got there first I would have stood no chance. I couldn't face another night on dog food alone. Mummy Cathy just said Daddy Kevin is daft. He put his freezing cold hands on her to show how cold it is out. She said he daft because he not wear a coat. Hang on; nobody put my coat on me. Do I not matter? Just because I have a natural fur lining, the wind still nips round the back of my ears. Michael not here yet. Chicken is safe. Daddy Kevin is off to somewhere called the gym. I wonder what he will bring me back. He always takes a big bag with him, so lots of room to put treats for me. I will let you know later.

That's tea over. They had smokey barbecued chicken. Except Michael who wanted fish with homemade chunky chips. Mummy Cathy and Daddy Kevin had half a chicken each. Greedy Daddy Kevin sat there pulling great big chunks of succulent chicken and throwing down his neck. Mummy Cathy only ate half of hers. I thought ooh I am going to get this. Oh no, Daddy Kevin grabbed it. I was mortified. Sat at table dribbling, sad eyes the works. I thought, nobody cares. I was going to get nothing and I really wanted that chicken. To make matters worse that Michael had a chocolate Jaffa cake sponge bar. Greedy or what. As always not even a speck of anything for me. All of a sudden a plate of chicken was put for me. Ooooh heaven. Mmmmmmmmm. All is forgiven, until next time. Mummy Cathy says I shouldn't be in the kitchen when they are eating because I always want feeding. Mummy Cathy should take this as a compliment. She is such a good cook, I cannot resist. Daddy Kevin is getting ready to out tonight. He says he is playing in a pool game with a long stick type thing. I am not sure how you swim with a stick?

He normally comes home all happy and chatty, funny thing is though he never takes a towel. Strange. I am going to have a cat nap now. Grrr cats.

How Lucky was my brother Mike. He was just getting ready to go back to his flat. He used to live with us but he moved in to his own place. Mummy Cathy used to get cross with him because he was always getting drunk and coming in late. Mummy Cathy and Daddy Kevin used to worry he was going to leave the door open and leave me outside. He used to have a bit of a beer belly but he has lost some of it now. I think he has been exercising like me. Spinning and rolling around the floor. Mummy Cathy says it's where he walks to work now. Anyway I have got side tracked again. As I said he was getting ready to go when suddenly he couldn't find his keys. We searched, well mummy Cathy and Michael searched. I watched, kind of bemused at what the panic was all about. Michael then rang his friend Holly and he had dropped it at her house. Panic over. Michael has gone now. Mummy Cathy says he now realises how important it is to look after his keys. Now I can feel the munchies creeping up on me, I shall have to give in and visit my food bowl. Munch munch munch.

I have just been woken up by my mummy Cathy sobbing her heart out. She was watching Paul O'Grady at Battersea dogs home. There was a white English bull dog on there. He looked very similar to me in the face. (Handsome chap he was). He has a cyst on his spine and cannot walk properly some of the time. They said it was inoperable. Mummy Cathy was sobbing like a baby. I had to give her a cuddle. She cries a lot at things on the telly. There was a film a couple of years ago with a Japanese dog. She cried for almost the whole film.

She had massive red swollen eyes by the end of it, and don't mention that War Horse film. Three times she has watched that and she still sobs. That's one of the reasons I love my mummy Cathy, she is so soppy and caring. She is going to make me cry in a minute and I am a big tough boy. Anyway that's enough crying mummy Cathy. I is trying to go back to sleep. I have bones to find and cats to chase. ZZZZZZZ

Morning all. Went outside for a pee. Got damp feet now. Not very nice. I slept sooo well last night. Must have had good dreams. Aaaah. Daddy Kevin came home just after I had comforted mummy Cathy. He didn't have his slippy shoes on though!! He was chatting about the pool again. He said he won 2 games and team won match. But what I still don't get is where his towel is!!!! Ha-ha just laughed at my sister's cat pic. Grrrr, I would have jumped over gate and chased that darn cat. Any way I have to start work now. Yawn, beds to test and all that. Yawn. Laters!!! Just remembered, Daddy Kevin comes home early today. Message to self. Beeeeee awake.

Well here we are again. The end of another week. Mummy Cathy and Daddy Kevin are both home and do not work weekends. This has its pluses and downfalls. It means I get to see more of them especially mummy Cathy but daddy Kevin goes off with his big bag with Gym. This reminds me, he didn't bring me anything back in that big bag yesterday. I think gym must have eaten it. Pig. Mummy Cathy gives me lots of cuddles and treats. Sometimes I help her tidy the kitchen, by picking up the oven gloves from the side and keeping them until she decides where to put them. I always get a biscuit for this. Though she is not always smiling at me. The best part is on a Saturday and Sunday morning. When mummy Cathy gets up she always sings a happy song to me. We call it the morning song. Also way before Clinton's cards brought out their boofles card range, mummy Cathy always called and still calls me her boofles woofles. I also look forward to my Sunday roast. MMMM homemade Yorkshire puds. Yummy. I am getting ahead of myself here. It's still only Friday. Mummy Cathy is cooking daddy Kevin scallops for his tea with a side salad, fancy mash with a parsley sauce. Daddy Kevin is a bit nervous about it. Don't know why. Anyway I have to go I can hear someone rustling around in the kitchen, they may be eating. I have worked extremely hard with my sofa/bed testing his week. I may have to work overtime at weekend. It is really exhausting jumping from one sofa to another all day long. I can't even sleep properly because mummy Cathy opens the blinds to let daylight in. Just because she has to go out to work. The light gets right in my eyes. Some people are just mean. Food Time.

While I have a spare 10 minutes I will tell you a little bit about me. I came to live with Mummy Cathy and Daddy Kevin when I was 4 months old. The 1st adoptive parents I had didn't want me. I was too young to know why. I am really glad now because I ended up striking gold. Cathy and Kevin are the best. They spoil me rotten. They always have. I was a gangly legged dog. All legs and ears and big. I was almost as big then as many full sized boxer dogs. I carried on growing and finally stopped at the size of roughly a Rottweiler. Mummy Cathy was asked once if I was a white rottie. I am not. I am a pure, white boxer dog with a good right hook. (Daddy Kevin has just commented on my spelling. Hang on, I am a dog.) Thankfully they had the foresight to insure me with Tesco. So far I have had plastic surgery on my eyes £1,500, due to my eyes being incorrect shape which could lead to blindness. I have also had my bits done, but even that wasn't simple. One of my testicles hadn't dropped so Paul (vet) had to put me to sleep and look for it so that both testicles could be removed. I am blushing now. No giggling. This was done firstly so that I wouldn't go looking for lady friend. Meanies, and secondly it was meant to calm me down. That didn't work. I is just hyper-active, not naughty. £500. I ate a rubber glove. What goes down apparently has to come back up. £200. I cut my tongue on a leaf and had to have stitches. £400. I also suffer with eczema, alopecia, and hay fever. I have regular anti-biotics and steroid tablets and hay fever tablets. Tablets cost around £100. Mummy Cathy nearly loses her hand putting tablets down my throat. Neither of us enjoys this. If it wasn't for Honey Bourne vets, (my favourite was Paul) mummy Cathy, Daddy Kevin and Tesco, I would be in a right state. I will have to leave it there for now. Daddy Kevin is calling me. It is walkies time. I hope it's not as cold as yesterday. It might be tea time when we get back. I hope so my tummy is rumbling......

Well what can I say about tea. Mummy Cathy is rather pleased with herself. She has cooked something called scallops, dolphins-potatoes? parsley sauce and a side salad. Daddy Kevin wasn't sure at first but said it was lovely. This is good but it also means none for me. Not good. Daddy Kevin did put some parsley sauce in my bowl which I chased around the kitchen floor. Why does my bowl never stay still? Mummy Cathy has just washed up. It is messy, bubbles everywhere. She then put out the recycle and took some bread outside. I fall for this every time. I think it is for me and get excited and always she throws it over the school car park for the dam birds. She'll be sorry when they poo on her washing. It's not all doom and gloom, she has promised me a piggy ear for working hard this week. Hey hey, that's a Brucie bonus. Daddy Kevin is now sat watching TV. His eyes are closing. I shall wait until they are shut and then jump on him. Only joking. When Mummy Cathy bought the scallop things. Apparently they come from the sea. They were still attached to their shells. Yuk. All slimy and nasty. It was like.... well I not allowed to say. Mummy Cathy is keeping the shells. Don't know why yet!!! Talking about the sea. I am not very keen on it. I have been to the sea-side a few times. I am told people love jumping in the sea and larking about. Not me. Not at all. Daddy Kevin has dragged me into the sea at Weston and a place called Bideford. It stung my eyes and I looked a pitiful sight. I ended up covered in sand and soooo tired. They made me run miles. They mistake me for a greyhound. Not looking forward to going back, except the doughnuts are nice. Anyway, I off to find my dinner now. I am still making up for the hunger strike.......

I am feeling a bit sorry for myself now. I told you earlier daddy Kevin was dragging me out for a walk. Well when I am, I really am well behaved. I walk to heel, I don't pull. That is unless I see something. Leaves blowing in the wind, birds. I jump a little bit and want to chase. Daddy Kevin stops me and off we go again. All good. If I see a cat I am a little bit naughty. I pull and try to get it. I even remember where I have seen them before and peer round hedges etc to see if they are still hiding from me. Now if I see another dog, it is a whole different story. I go mad. I jump in the air, I twist my lead, trying to get free. All I want to do is go and play with the other dog. People look at me as if I am a real bad dog. I am not, I just get over excited. When I was a puppy, I used to be scared of little yappy dogs. Mummy Cathy and my brother Jon were coming home from walking me when a man with a white westie stopped to chat with them. The dog kept barking at me. I was so scared I actually peed myself. Oh the embarrassment. I can't believe I have just told you all this. So I think when I get all excited and act naughty. Really I am just showing I am not scared now. I think I am really though. Anyway back to why I am feeling sorry for myself. When we were out for my walk tonight. There were lots of dogs and I was naughty. Whilst I was jumping and twisting on my lead, somehow it pinched my lip and made it bleed. Mummy Cathy has had to clean it and bathe it with dettol. Also my hay fever was making me itch so I have had my hay fever tablets and my anti-biotics rammed down my throat. I off to sleep now. Daddy Kevin has gone for a soak in the bath, Urgh. That's a story for another day. Mummy Cathy is putting washing into the washing machine. Me I am going to sleep. Good Night all. Sleep tight. Don't let the bed bugs bite. X

I have to be quick this time. I have been banned from using the p.c. Reason being, I woke mummy Cathy and daddy Kevin 5 times before they got up. Whoops. I was awake I thought they should be too. Mummy Cathy was the crossest I think. Sorreeeee. Mummy Cathy is really kind and selfless. In the mornings she sets 2 alarms, one for daddy Kevin at 5am and then one for herself. Daddy Kevin wears a cochlear for his hearing which he takes out at night. This means he wouldn't hear an alarm clock. He has a vibrating clock. It goes wibbly wobbly, wibbly wobbly. It is to go under a pillow but he doesn't like it. So mummy Cathy wakes him up. Just before Christmas mummy Cathy was poorly. She had a real sadness behind her eyes. Daddy Kevin, me obviously and my sister Michelle and her brilliant family have helped mummy Cathy a lot. Even when she was poorly, she still managed to wake daddy Kevin. That's the trouble with mummy Cathy she always puts everyone else before her. She feels really guilty that my brother Mikey has moved out. People say she kicked him out. It wasn't like that, there was more to it. She kind of did but not in a horrible way. He needed to see what the real world was like and stand on his own two feet. Mummy Cathy and Daddy Kevin helped him move in, the flat was scrubbed through, pictures hung. Everything sorted. Mikey was actually at work. When he came home it was all sorted. They gave him tons of stuff he needed for his kitchen. Mummy Cathy still gives him bags and bags of shopping so that he won't starve. It is nice now for mummy as Mike does pop round to visit and has meals with us. This makes mummy Cathy smile and be happy. Anyway as I was saying, I am in the doghouse for a while. It won't last. I will wag my tail and creep round them both. They cannot be mad at me for long. I am just too clever for them. It's a good job mummy Cathy and daddy Kevin don't read this all of the time or I would be in more trouble. Ha-ha. Do you know what, all of that up and down the stairs disturbing my parents, I am feeling tired. I think it must be nap time. Catch you laters......

A massive well done to my sister on her bread making. Mummy Cathy says you can't beat home made. I am out of the dog house now. I was poorly earlier and had to make myself sick. (Hope u not eating your bread Chellsey). I convinced them that was why I woke them up the 5 times in the early hours of this morning. Really I just wanted to get them up. Blimey, it is hail stoning outside. Like bullets hitting the garden. Glad daddy Kevin not dragging me out in this. Daddy Kevin was a proper lazy bones today. He didn't come downstairs until almost 2pm. Mummy Cathy didn't seem to mind, she said he works hard building them car bits. Mummy Cathy even made him 2 sausage, egg and tomato sandwiches. Obviously I was well even to scrounge for that. He has now gone with his big bag to see gym again. He seems to like gym., whoever or whatever he is. I am a little bit scared of the hail stones, they made me jump!!! I am a big baby, in need of a cuddle. Mummy Cathy has been doing house work all day. Hoovering, mopping, polishing etc. This includes wiping doggy drool from cupboard doors. Sorreee! She has even done all veg for today and tomorrows dinners. She is making the batter for her yorkies in a minute and a rhubarb crumble. Like I said she has been busy. Me I have been working hard, testing the sofa for napping possibilities. It has passed all tests. Daddy Kevin is back now so I have to go and wag my tail and get excited. You never know he may be hungry......

Well another day almost coming to an end for me. I have had to watch mummy Cathy cooking tea (gammon mmmm), she also made a chocolate sponge. I don't know where she has found the time to do everything today. Daddy Kevin has been like me today, Lazy. Ha-ha. I haven't even had a walk today yet. He is sat now playing on his phone. He does this a lot. It gets on mummy Cathy's nerves sometimes. I hear her tutting at him. She has told him he is wasting his weekend. Whoops. Sounds like he may be in the doghouse now. I shall give him some tips on how to get out of it. I was thinking earlier whilst I was in the garden (in between rain storms). I had had a pee against mummy Cathy's spinning washing line thing. My thought was, daddy Kevin told me off for sniffing my pee. The thing is how do I know who's pee it is if I don't sniff it. My brain is so busy with important things (mainly to do with food) I normally forget as soon as I have peed and so I have to check. You might be thinking who else pee's in our back garden. Probably no one else, but you can never be too sure. Everyone is saying well done to Wigan, so well done Wigan. They have won a F.A. cup. What's an F.A. cup? Daddy Kevin betted on Wigan to win 2-1. Right team but wrong score. Oh well in the bin it goes. Mummy Cathy laughed and said Again. Anyway I am going to have to end now as it is my bedtime and I am already yawning. Night night all......

Well what a fun morning I have had. I slept in my brother Mikey's old room last night. It has been decorated and has nice things in it for me to play with. When I woke this morning I noticed what mummy Cathy calls the shoe rack. I didn't know they was called shoes to me they are tug toys. I found daddy Kevin's flip flops. I sat outside their bedroom door, they closed it last night. Don't know why? When mummy Cathy got up, she is always first on the weekend, she burst out laughing. I knew it was a good game. She called me into the bedroom and then, for no reason, daddy Kevin snatched it off me. Hey that wasn't fair; if he wanted to play he should get his own flip flop. I went back to the toy rack and got the other flip flop. Ha, I am not stupid. Well I wasn't giving this one up so easily, or so I thought because the next thing I know daddy Kevin has grabbed this one off me also. I am going to have to teach him the rules of this game. What are the rules again? Anyway mummy Cathy is now hoovering upstairs, 2 spare rooms, bathroom and toilet. I keep out of the way by lying in their bedroom on floor. Lying on the floor, how humiliating. Daddy Kevin has gone in the room where he comes out wet. I don't like that room. Mummy Cathy made me go in there once. She hauled me into what she called the bath and went on to try and drown me with bubbles and water. I tried to escape a few times. There was water everywhere. Mummy Cathy was drenched; the floor was like a paddling pool. She has never done it again. She now does it on warm days in the garden with the hose pipe. I hate this also. If I was meant to like water I would be a duck or a dogfish, which I am not. I have wandered away from the story again, sorry. So daddy Kevin was in the shower and mummy was hoovering. While no one was watching me and mummy Cathy had taken the hoover in to their bedroom I sneaked back and retrieved the flip flop from the toy rack. Daddy Kevin clearly had given up and ha, I win. Whilst we are talking about the upstairs part of our house. I am not stupid. Every time I peep into the toilet room. Daddy Kevin says noooo to me. Does he really think I would drink from the toilet? I don't think so. Oooooh my god, some of the smells that come from that room I would not, definitely would not drink from the toilet. I have 2 bowls which I drink from; I do not need a third. Yuk!!!!! Dinner is now cooking and I have to go guard the oven.........

Well what a busy day I have had today. Firstly the flip flop game this morning, and I have stolen mummy Cathy's slippers a couple of times this afternoon. It was payback for not sharing her dinner with me. Mummy Cathy was cross with me for what I said about the aroma coming from the toilet. So just to clarify, when mummy Cathy uses the loo it has the fragrant scent of roses and lavender coming from it. Daddy Kevin is a man so it doesn't matter to him, plus he has no sense of smell. My brother Mikey came here again today for his lunch and to watch footie. Daddy Kevin has taken him home and gone to my sister's house to drop off magazine. My niece Shannon loves to read about the soaps. Also a massive good luck to Shanny Panny on her SATS this week. I wanted to come in car but wasn't allowed. I went out in the front garden to help mummy Cathy with the weeding. I got sent in for peeing on plants and eating other plants. I was only trying to help. Daddy Kevin shared his crumble with me, yummy. Michael had chocolate cake, he didn't share. I told you about all of my health problems the other day. Well I forgot to tell you about my spots. Like teenagers get spots and boils, so do I. The anti biotics help, but I still get them. I had a big spot under my eye today. Mummy Cathy cleaned it with dettol and burst it for me. She gets all of the good jobs. I also suffer with conjunctivitis a lot. Daddy Kevin has to put drops in to my eyes for this. I am tired now and going to sleep. The end of a busy Sunday. Night Night.....

Hello. Have you all wondered where I have been? Well mummy Cathy and Daddy Kevin went off to work and left me on my own. I have had a sad old day today. I had to ring our home landline number (remember I work from home) to ring work and tell them I wouldn't be bed testing today as I had a belly ache. By the time daddy Kevin came home, I hope no one is eating, I had been sick everywhere. Daddy Kevin cleared it up but left the rug scrubbing for mummy Cathy. I am looking and feeling very sorry for myself. I am hoping it is just a 24 hr bug as cannot afford another day off work. Daddy Kevin has said my brother Jon and his partner Sarah are expecting a little girl. Ahhhhhh that is nice news. Poor old mummy Cathy, she has come in from work, scrubbed the rug, peeled tatoes and put tea on. Daddy Kevin, he has gone to see gym again. Yep with his big bag. Mummy Cathy is making sarnies for work tomorrow now. I think daddy Kevin should do tea tomorrow. I haven't even got the energy today to go and play the flip flop game. That is how poorly I am. I think they will have to call 999 soon. I will make do with cuddles. Hope I feel better when they eating tea. I off to sleep now. Mummy Cathy says sleep is the best medicine.......

Hello all. This is mummy Cathy again. Troy has had to take another sick day today. He was too tired today to even wag his tail. Daddy Kevin will be with him soon and see how he is. Hopefully he will have slept his bug off. Let u know how he is later.

Hey guess what. I am all better. When daddy Kevin came home from work I was back to my usual self, looking for food and jumping about all over him. I even took my pink baby to see him. This is something I normally only do for mummy Cathy. In case you are wondering what my babies are. There is a pink piggy, a yellow duckie and a black cat. They used to have stuffing in them and squeaked. They must have been faulty because within a few minutes they all had holes in and the stuffing was coming out. Apparently this is dangerous for me if I eat it so mummy Cathy managed to pull out all of the stuffing and now I have 3 flat babies. I love them to bits. Whenever mummy Cathy comes in I always greet her with one of my babies, I also sleep with them. They are like my comforters. So when mummy Cathy came in from work tonight, I went mad. I was jumping round like a new born lamb. Then I couldn't find pink baby. He was on the kitchen floor where I had dropped him earlier. Mummy Cathy and daddy Kevin are so relieved I am better. I still have a bit of a sore throat and my chest hurts from retching yesterday. Mummy Cathy says that will be gone in a day or two. Back to work for me tomorrow. Those beds won't test themselves you know. My sister got knocked off her bike yesterday by a very nasty, rude lady. She didn't help my sister or check she was ok or nothing. Grrrrrr. If I see her I will chew her leg off for you Chellesy. Grrrr. Daddy Kevin is off to the pool again tonight. Remember the pool where he doesn't take a towel but takes a big stick. Weird. Anyway as I have work tomorrow and am still a bit tired I will say nite nite . Grrrrr nasty lady. Glad you ok Chellesy

Well another days work over. About what mummy Cathy said earlier, the name Alice Morse isn't his real name. I am much better today. Felt a bit iffy first thing but ok now. I greeted mummy Cathy with my black baby today. I haven't played with that one for a while. Daddy Kevin has gone with his big bag again to see gym. I am going to get to the bottom of this gym one day. I wonder if mummy Cathy knows gym. She hasn't said, so I guess not. I can smell chicken in the oven, mmmm. Hope it's for me. Bet it's not though. Mummy Cathy touched on me having to go to the vets if I didn't get better. Ooooh I wish I had known. I love the vets. My favourite vet is Paul. He left our surgery (honeybourne) last year. He was the best. I used to make myself poorly just to see Paul. I used to sit in the waiting room, as soon as I saw Paul; all four of my legs would be trying to run. The floor would be slippy and I just never seemed to move. I was like Scooby doo. The day Paul left he came into the surgery especially to see me. Daddy Kevin and mummy Cathy bought him a bottle of wine and I wrote him a poem in a card. I do miss him. Still I am better now so no trip to the vet. My niece Shannon is getting married soon, in a few years, too someone called Harry Styles. I don't know who he is but he not good enough for my Shanny. She says he is in a pop group. Ooooh, I wonder if I could be a page boy. If he misbehaves I could chew his leg off. Grrrrr. Message to Shanny. Work hard at your exams at school. You don't want to end up a bed tester like me do you? I am sounding like mummy Cathy, handing out advice. Lol. Anyway it is nearly night nights time for me so I say night night......

Hello. Sorry I haven't been on f/b for last few days but mummy Cathy who does my typing, (you didn't really think I did it myself did you) has come home from work with migraine and gone straight to bed. That was Wednesday and Thursday. She is much better today. She has just been on phone again to virgin mobile. Some woman in the Philippine's has just had an ear bashing. Daddy Kevin went to the pool again last night, still no towel. When he came home from the pool on Tuesday he was really wet. He said it was because it was raining. I am not so sure. Anyway when daddy Kevin went to the pool last night I went upstairs and found mummy Cathy. I checked she was ok and then went to sleep on the floor in corner of her bedroom. Anyone who is interested, I am much better now and back to my usual self. Daddy Kevin came home from work today and we played the trainer game, it is similar to the flip flop game but with a trainer. I am so easily pleased and occupied. I love playing shoe type games. When I was younger I always got the rules wrong. I used to think you had to eat the shoe or slipper. I have learnt with age to play the game correctly. Nanny and grampy Haysome came to see me today. Daddy Kevin thinks they came to see him but I know different. They looked at all the vegetables growing in the garden. Daddy Kevin made them a cup of tea. Mummy Cathy came home from work, she didn't get so much as a glass of water. Aaaah poor mummy Cathy!!!! Daddy Kevin did cook tea today though. He did fancy jacket potatoes and fancy strawberries and ice-cream for pudding. They didn't share with me at all. I did get a piece of cake though, yummy. I hope Shannon has finished her exams now. A big woof woof to Shannon Joseph and Eleanor, hope you all being as good as I am. I am going to sleep now as it is past my bed time. Night night. Mummy Cathy has said she hopes it a nice day tomorrow so that maybe she and Michelle can bugger off to the car boot.

Hello. I am at nanny Brenda's and Grampy Dennis's at the moment. I like it at their house because they have a big garden I can run around. They do grumble when I run through their flowers though. They have tried to stop me by putting ladders and chairs round borders to stop me. We will see. For the moment it not matter as I shattered from running round garden. Mummy Cathy and daddy Kevin kept hiding from me

They were hiding behind a shed. Even though I know they were there it still made me jump. I am led in the conservatory at moment panting. The garden is on a slope and so it is tiring running up and down. Kevin is talking about setting up a face book account for Nanny Brenda. I will have to be careful what I write in future. There are so many things I could be doing here but I am trying to be good. It is difficult.

All I keep hearing is Troy go out and run, who they think I am Usain Bolt or Linford Christie. Dogs next door barking. I had to run out and check they weren't going to trespass in Nanny Brenda's garden. I have pee'd for the second time against the fuscias. Ha they won't keep nagging for me to go in garden now. Ha-ha. Anyway I off for a wander now. Catch ya laters.....

OMG. I think I am dying. I have been running up and down garden. I am watching daddy Kevin on grampy Dennis's laptop. He is setting up face book. Blimey it might be a long afternoon. It is like Bill and Ben, listening to them disagreeing about things. No tolerance levels from daddy Kevin. Still they are nagging me to go running so I will leave them in peace. Mummy Cathy says they will be ages....

Like I said. They are still sorting face book. They forgot the password. How can you forget? When you have only just added it. I have been out in garden with mummy Cathy. Much more fun. Daddy Kevin has forgotten I am here. He will be sorry later I will jump all over him. Ha-ha Mummy Cathy has got a custard tart now. yummy...

Wow I have just seen a beautiful pic of Eleanor. Aah she is lovely. I had such a tiring afternoon running around. Oh and Chellesy mummy Cathy and daddy Kevin shared their custard tarts with me. Mummy Cathy is watching the Eurovision; she said someone called Bonnie Tyler was crap. Mummy Cathy said she was our entrant. I could have howled better. I think we will get nil points. Lol. Daddy Kevin went into the front garden and did a bit of weeding. I got sent in. I kept finding bark chippings and eating it. Apparently it isn't for eating. Daddy Kevin then planted some fox gloves, sweet peas and lupin seeds for mummy Cathy. Mummy Cathy has put my bed covers in the washing machine.

She said they were disgustingly dirty. She says I am a scruffle bunny. What is a scruffle bunny? I thought I was her boofles woofles. I am not sure about scruffle bunnies, but I do like chocolate bunnies. I shall dream about chasing chocolate bunnies around Nanny Brenda's garden. The noisy dogs next door shan't get em. Grrrr. Night night. Sweet dreams. xxxxxx xxxxxxxxxxxxxxxxxxxxxxxxxxxx

Well mummy Cathy was proper lazy this morning or should I say this afternoon. Her excuse for getting up after 12pm was, mummy Cathy and Daddy Kevin were watching TV last night and the clock said 12.10. Ages after daddy Kevin checked the time on his phone and it was 2.10. Their clock in lounge had stopped. Mummy Cathy hardly ever stays up this late. She says it is because she is getting old. Well she is 50. Ha-ha. She will be cross now. Sorreeee. I tried waking them up but it didn't work. When mummy Cathy did finally get up, I was napping. When I woke mummy Cathy sang my morning songs to me. Even though it was the afternoon. I did not mind. I still did my wiggle dance and wagged my tail. Mummy Cathy washed my bed covers yesterday. They are back on my beds and smelly foofoo. This means smelling lovely and fresh. Daddy Kevin took me for a walk to see my sister Michelle and her family. We get Shanny a TV mag every week because she loves to read about Eastenders. Mummy Cathy is cooking the dinner. Mmmmmmm roast chicken today. I am looking forward to this as I am starving. I have only had 2 bonio biscuits and a piece of stale french stick oh and some toast I scrounged from daddy Kevin so far today. My ribs will soon be poking out. I am growing weaker every second!!!! I think I may have 40 winks now and conserve the bit of energy I have left till I have my chicken dinner.....

I have been sunning myself in the garden this afternoon. Could have done with one of them ice-creams Shanny and Joey had. Yummmmm. Mummy Cathy puts ice cubes in my water bowl, it is not the same. Mummy Cathy and Daddy Kevin have been having a sort out in wardrobes and loft. They are getting rid of so much stuff. Mummy Cathy says it is all crap and needs to be gone. Mummy Cathy was upset earlier, something to do with my big brother. I am cheering her up as I can do no wrong in her eyes. I am going to teach Joey all of my tricks. Joey is my new best friend. He didn't used to like me, but we get on good now. Fun to be had in the future!!! I had a massive chicken dinner. I even ate my carrots, they were mashed up though. I was so full I just flopped down in the garden, that is how I came to be sun bathing. Mummy Cathy is telling me to hurry up as it is my bedtime and I have work tomorrow. I will say good night all otherwise she might ground me. I can't have that because I need to go outside to pee etc. Night night......XXXX

Hello. I have had a quiet day today. Mondays aren't my favourite day. Back to work an all that. People do not realise how tiring bed testing is. I have a job to keep my eyes open in the afternoon!!! Hey sis was the ice-cream nice? Did you save me some? Someone upset my sis earlier, Grrrrrr. Mummy Cathy and me just had scrambled egg on toast. Mmmmmm. Daddy Kevin's gone to see Gym with his big bag again. Who is he?...

Following on from a warning Mummy Cathy told you about the other day about a teenage lad calling himself Alice Morse on f/b and trying to befriend strangers. He even asked me to be his friend the other day. Alice, Alice who the fcuk is Alice. I guess he must have gender issues like Kasey on waterloo road. Any way there are ants to follow in garden....

Well I am getting ready for bed now. Let's be honest, all I have to do is decide where to lie down. Nanny Brenda rang mummy Cathy tonight. Grampy Dennis won a trophy playing golf. Well done grampy Dennis. Nanny Brenda went to see a quilt show yesterday. I am a bit muddled. What do quilts do in a show? She had a good time, so they must have been okay. I got fed up earlier following the ants. They tickle my nose. Daddy Kevin is having a bath now in the wet room that I do not like. There is no way I am going in there ever again. I was in the room that used to be my brother Mikes and mummy Cathy frightened me. She kept moving the door. I didn't see her hand doing it and got scared and ran out. I will have to stop watching those paranormal activity films. Mummy Cathy laughed at me. I can't help being a sensitive type. Anyways, time for sleepys. Nite nite folks. Till we meet again.......

Woof woof. I am on my lunch break. Sofa testing makes me really hungry. I might also have a little nap before I get back to work. I am lucky working from home. No travelling costs either. This is good because where the hell would I keep my bus fare. Is that what a doggy bag is for? As it is father's day soon I will have to start exercising my brain as to what I can get him. More exercise. Grrrrr....

Everyone that knows my sis, Michelle Fraser, please send her a hug. Thank you. She deserves it. Love you Lelly Bob. xxxxxxxxxxxxxxxxxx

Well that's tea over. Mummy Cathy and daddy Kevin had pork. I had little bit. yummy. Daddy Kevin is trying to take me for a walk. I always run around the table in the kitchen pretending I don't want to go. This game always makes mummy Cathy and daddy Kevin laugh at me as I wag my tail. Mummy Cathy still has a cold. She has nearly lost her voice. Daddy Kevin said, only nearly. Ha-ha. Anyway off to walkies....

I got caught napping on the job today. Mummy Cathy came home from work poorly and found me having 40 winks on sofa. Of course I jumped up wagging my taily. I was so pleased to see her. I don't think she will dock my wages. Mummy Cathy went to bed for a while. She is up now. Led on the sofa watching a film. Here's a puzzle for u. what has 4 I's but cannot see anything. Answers later....

Ha-ha. Gotcha. It is Mississippi KFC sounds yummy. Daddy Kevin said if you want the cage, it is yours. No payment needed. Mummy Cathy is feeling a lot better now. My sister gave me a big bag of bones a while ago and mummy Cathy put them in freezer. Mmmmm I have just had one. A treat before bedtime I was practising the trainer game earlier but mummy Cathy spoilt it by taking trainer off me. How can I get better if I not allowed to practise? When daddy Kevin came home I wanted to show him how good I was getting but he went and put trainers on. Game over. I been told it bedtime now. Dream time....X

Good afternoon. I am on my lunch break. No one was watching so I ate my lunch early. Mummy Cathy had given me a bone for lunch so u get why I couldn't wait. The best part is as I have already eaten I am going to have a nap. Mummy Cathy is happy; the weather forecast for weekend is looking ok. She just hopes her cold is gone. Anyway nap time...

How sad reading on f/b about the young soldier and father. A little boy who will never know the love of his daddy. Terrorism or a brutal murder. How does this happen in a civilised country. All of our heroic armed forces are deployed to make the world a safer place, but who is making our country feel safe. Our hero's should be able to be safe and relaxed when they are back home and not have to be on alert as they are when in a war zone. Our police, our government are letting us all down, but most

I won't be saying much tonight. Mummy Cathy has been coughing a lot tonight. her throat must be red raw. Daddy Kevin has told her to stop talking. I think though that is just for his benefit. He is getting ready for his pool games tonight. He has said something about an umbrella. This is really strange. Firstly he goes off to a pool, with his long stick thing and no towel and now with an umbrella. Why would you take an umbrella to a pool. See, I said it is strange. I am getting really good at the trainer game. I have had a good practice today, soon I will be invincible. Haha. daddy Kevin took a big box of cd's (music discs is what he said they were) to the charity shop today. They used to belong to my big brother Jon, but he didn't want them. I am feeling sleepy now so I think I will go to sleep. An early night I think. Night night all......

What fun I have had today. I stole mummy Cathys slipper and then left it for her to find. That way she laughs at me and I am not told off. Mummy Cathy is still feeling crappy. she keeps coughing. You should see the stuff that comes out of her mouth and nose. Whoops hope you not eating your picnic shellsey. She won't be happy at me saying this. I hope she gets better soon!!! Hey its walkies time. I will try to be good

Haha. I played a new game today. I have called it the flip flop game. it is similar to the trainer and slipper game but with a flip flop. You get the gist. Mummy Cathy was sat in the garden this afternoon, she got up to put some washing on the line and takes more washing in. all the time coughing like she was choking. Daddy Kevin was sat also in garden reading paper. Mummy Cathy carried on with her washing,

Still coughing and spluttering. She then folded all washing up and put in basket to be put upstairs. When she eventually sat back down, still coughing. Daddy Kevin looked up from his paper and said, you alright. I thought mummy Cathy was going to punch him. I hid my eyes under my paws....Mummy Cathy just said bloody ME

I have been a bit poorly tonight. I think it is probably too much sun. I shall stay in shade more tomorrow. I just want to be a brown boxer for a while. Mummy Cathy dyes her fur, why can't I. God, it's not fair. I am going to my room now to sulk......

I might have to be a deserter and go AWOL. How can I go AWOL when I cannot go out without a lead? I will have to persuade daddy Kevin to come with me. Watch this space.....

Mummy Cathy is going out in a minute with my sis, chellesy. When she gets back it is time for school. I am starting to worry. I thought she was joking yesterday. Will I get detention? Oh god, probably!!! Do they still give the cane? I don't mind if they give me the slipper. I am good at the slipper game. This is all daddy Kevin's fault. I shall tell him that he has to come to school with me and be trained also.....

OMG! I am just back from doggy school. I am so tired. Mummy Cathy was so proud of me. I ran around, came when she called and sat when told. Daddy Kevin tried to order me around but no chance. He is so softly spoken, mummy Cathy says he has no authority in his voice. Mummy Cathy says I passed today's tests with flying colours but daddy Kevin failed miserably. No detention for me. I have to practise at home now.....

I shall dream of Freedom.......X

I am tired today. All of this going to school and having lessons is tiring. I had to go again today with daddy Kevin. It was raining again. No coat. Daddy Kevin had his coat on. It not matter about poor little me. Daddy Kevin isn't brave like mummy Cathy. He took me to a babies park. SHHHHHH I am not meant to go in the babies park. Daddy Kevin takes me there because it is enclosed. Any babies reading this, I never pee's or pooh's in there. I have nearly cut my feet on the beer cans mind you. What you babies doing drinking in the park I do not know. Haven't you got cots at home to drink in? We didn't stay too long because it was wet and well daddy Kevin had to get home because mummy Cathy had told him to turn the oven on. Daddy Kevin mind you is a proper naughty person. Mummy Cathy has hardly seen him this week. He has gone swimming with his stick on Tuesday night, Wednesday night and again tonight. He isn't even giving his stick chance to dry out!!! Last night he stayed up really late watching telly. Kept me awake because he was munching. I couldn't sleep with the chance of some cheesy balls going begging. Today as he didn't have to go to work he didn't get up until after 1pm. Lazy or what. I tried to wake him up earlier but no luck. Daddy Kevin is going for a long walk with his dad (Grampy Dennis) tomorrow. In between walking they hit little white balls about using funny stick things. Daddy Kevin seems to like stick games. This game isn't in a pool though it is on grass. I would like to have a go but daddy Kevin says I am not allowed. I think he is worried I might beat him. Daddy Kevin and grampy Dennis quite often loose balls. I think this is because when they are walking and talking they forget what they are doing. Apparently, they have to chase the little white ball down a hole. Daddy Kevin takes a lot of different sticks with him in a massive bag. It seems daft taking all that heavy stuff with you on a walk!!!! Men, they are strange. I had an accident earlier. No not that kind of accident. When mummy Cathy came home from work, I was so excited. I took yellow baby to meet her and ran into the garden and dropped him. I came in and had a big cuddle and forgot about yellow baby. He is soaking wet now from being out in the rain and mummy Cathy has pegged him on the washing line. Does this make me a bad parent? Never mind, I still have pink and black baby to sleep with and cuddle. Night night......

Wow, I have the biggest news ever. Really, ever. Mummy Cathy and daddy Kevin are getting me a new brother or sister. Not a baby or nothing. Mummy Cathy is way too old for all that stuff. No they are getting me a doggy brother or sister. I am so happy. We went to do my lessons at the park by Welsh road earlier. Daddy Kevin was so scared. Talking about daddy Kevin, there was a typo error last night. It was meant to say his red arms matched his red head. Even more so today. Hehehe.

In the park, daddy Kevin nervously took my lead off. Like a bullet from a gun I was gone. Mummy Cathy called me and I obeyed. I am soooo good. There were a few scary moments when daddy Kevin nearly had to go home and change his boxers. I saw a few dogs and each time I ran as fast as my legs would go. Mummy Cathy was calling me but nothing was stopping me. When I reached the dogs, I did nothing. I just wanted to look at them. Most of my new found friends didn't mind me by them, but they was one scrawny little rat on a rope. It was horrible. I was so scared. I was barking and snarling at me. Its owner picked it up but it jumped out of his arms. He went to say something to mummy Cathy but changed his mind when he saw the look on her face. Daddy Kevin gave me a cuddle. Silly thing is, one bite and I could have eaten it whole. I then carried on running around and having so much fun. I don't like water normally but there are a couple of ponds there. Guess what, I only went in them. I drank the water, tadpoles as well. I had legs thick in mud. I went rock climbing like a mountain lion. I am so clever. I have missed out on so much being a silly boy. I promise I will listen in the future. Anyway, back to my new brother or sister. Mummy Cathy has spoken with Battersea dogs home and registered and also with the animal shelter in Cheltenham. Daddy Kevin is up on a big ladder at the moment cleaning the guttering on our house. You should see the muck he has cleaned out. He is also cleaning the conservatory roof because it is covered in something called moss. When new mummys are having new babies they clean and call it nesting. Maybe this is what daddy Kevin is doing before our new family member arrives. It is all sooo exciting but I am sleepy now. Oh I have just thought. Where will my new brother or sister sleep? I am lucky. I have 3 or 4 beds to sleep on but they won't have any. Will I have to share? Will I have to share my toys, my babies are MINE!!! My food and treats are MINE!!!! Not even up for discussion. Mummy Cathy and daddy Kevin will have to sort this out, maybe the new dog will have a kennel in the garden. That would probably be the best. Night night............

Remember yesterday I told you I was having a new brother or sister. It is now official. I am having a brother. He is six years old and called Tyson. Mummy Cathy says he doesn't look like a Tyson so they are changing it to either Percius (Percy for short) or sonny. He is a bit poorly at the moment. He has to have an operation this week to remove a mamory gland (a nipple). Also he needs his teeth cleaned and maybe a couple removed. He is very thin and under weight. He has been in a dog pound in Ireland and was going to be put down. The dogs trust have saved him. He will be with us in a couple of weeks. I have been told he is not as handsome as me or as big as me. I am going to meet him on Wednesday to see if we will get along together. Mummy Cathy and daddy Kevin have then got to go to an adoption meeting next Saturday. We have just had our roast dinner, roast beef and yorkshire pudding. Mummy Cathy has just washed up. My other brother Mikey is here. Grrrrr less meat for me. Nice to see him though. He has had his Bieber hair cut off and now has a skinny head. I didn't recognise him at first. Daddy Kevin is up the ladder again cleaning out the gutters at front of house now. Mummy Cathy doesn't like him up ladders, it scares her. I don't like it either but only because I cannot see him. I have just been told I will have to share all of my treats, which is not fair. Maybe my new brother will not like treats or toys or anything else that is mine. I will have to be nice to him as I have been lucky with mummy Cathy and daddy Kevin. If they hadn't of adopted me, I could have ended up like Percius/Sonny. Not in Ireland though. I am sure we will get along. It will be nice to have my brother to play with in the park. Any way tomorrow is a work day so I need to get m y beauty sleep. Hey I will be able to share my job with Percius/Sonny. Night night.......

I forgot to say Percius/Sonny is a white boxer just like me but smaller. It is lovely and sunny out but obviously I am working. We have the adoption people coming tomorrow to check us out. How exciting I will have to be good. Wednesday I get to meet my brother. Mummy Cathy and daddy Kevin are coming with me. I am so nervous. It is time to go back to sleep now, whoops I mean work....

Wow I am so nervous. We have the doggy social services coming tomorrow. I have got to be on my best behaviour. Mummy Cathy has hoovered. Mummy Cathy is doing a late shift tomorrow as well so that she can here with me in case either me or daddy Kevin are naughty. Maybe we will have my new brother at weekend. That would be so exciting. I have to go to sleepy byes now ready for tomorrow. good night......

I am late tonight. Mummy Cathy has been busy since she came home from work. I was really well behaved when the doggy social services came today. They were happy with all of my doggy beds. I will have to share now. I am being taken to meet Percy tomorrow for the 1st time. I am really nervous. I hope he likes me. What if we don't get on? Mummy Cathy says we will get on lovely together. I hope so. night night ....

What a disappointing day I had today. Mummy Cathy and daddy Kevin took me to see my brother (Percy) today. We were meant to have had a play time today. The meany people who is staying with forgot and sent him to the vets. He has had surgery today. He has had the snip (ouch), I had that done when I was younger. I also had a testicle that hadn't dropped. Sore!!!, He also has to have a mammary gland (nipple) removed and his teeth sorted. I bet he is feeling rough now. AAAH!!!! So now I have to wait until Saturday to meet Percy. Mummy Cathy was upset this morning. My brother Jon said some things to her he shouldn't have. He should listen to himself before he speaks. Apparently mummy Cathy collapsed at work today because she was so upset. They wanted to call Daddy Kevin but mummy Cathy wouldn't let them. Mummy Cathy is ok now. She has been to see my sis and her family. She had fun there. Alan's brother Mike wants a girlfriend and has asked mummy Cathy to help him get one. So if anyone can help please please do so. When I saw mummy Cathy at lunchtime she had the sadness back behind her eyes. Big thank you to my Sis for getting her to smile again. 3 more big sleeps till I see Percy, night night.......

Meant to say 4 more big sleeps till I see Percy

I have just popped into town. I hope no-one has seen me as mummy Cathy works in town. I might be in trouble. Hopefully not. Daddy's day is coming up and I have been saving my wages to get a pressie for daddy Kevin. I have to rush home now before daddy Kevin gets back from seeing gym. He still takes that big bag with him. No food ever comes out of it.......

Hey guess what. I was busted. Mummy Cathy came home from work and asked what I was doing in town on my own. She said you are only 6 years old and I have been told over and over not to go out on my own. Hang on a minute. I am old enough to be working all day as a sofa and bed tester. Is this not a real job or am I being exploited? I am 42 in doggy years. Mummy Cathy says this doesn't count. Plus I got the weekend wrong. It is not father's day this weekend but next weekend. Mummy Cathy was also cross because I had sneaked out without telling Daddy Kevin I was going anywhere. She said if I had been in an accident or dog napped we wouldn't have known where to start looking. Mummy Cathy and daddy Kevin, I am sorreeeeee!. X I won't do it again. (Until the next time). Daddy Kevin text mummy Cathy with a really mixed up text about the doggy home and my brother to be Percy. Daddy Kevin says they rang and said he is poorly with a bad heart. Mummy Cathy is really worried as this may mean we cannot have him. They are closed now so mummy Cathy will have to ring them tomorrow. I do hope he is alright. Get well soon Percy.Mikes girlfriend hunt isn't doing too well at the moment. As far as I know not one female has shown any interest. My sis has shown her friends the photo but not mummy Cathy's comments. Shellsey, how will they know he is looking for a girlfriend!!!!! Mike if you are reading this, chin up mate. We will keep trying for you. Anyway I am tired now from all my gallivanting. Night night........

Massive disappointment for me today. Mummy Cathy has just rang me to tell me I cannot go and see Percy tomorrow. He has bad kennel cough and is on anti-biotics. Although I have been the kennel cough vaccine apparently it is not a good idea for us to mix when Percy is unwell. Percy also has an irregular heart beat. Poor Percy. He was too poorly on Wednesday to have his ops so Percy has still got that to go through. It doesn't look like he will be coming to live with me anytime soon.

Mummy Cathy and Daddy Kevin are still going to visit him tomorrow. Get well soon Percy!!! X

Mummy Cathy and daddy Kevin went to see Percy this afternoon. They took him to a field and played with him and gave him some of MY doggy treats. I didn't really mind, but would have like to have been there to tell Percy he can't have them all! Mummy Cathy said he seemed a bit better and that he looked like he had put a bit of weight on. They sat on the grass with Percy while he had treats. Daddy Kevin said Percy cuddled up to mummy Cathy as if he had known her forever. He gave her kisses and led across her lap. Now I don't want to enforce the big brother thing. But she was my mummy Cathy first and my daddy Kevin first also. I am going to have to set some rules down I think. Mummy Cathy has said I will always be their number one baby. It is just that Percy has had a tough life and hasn't been as lucky as me and deserves a few hugs. This time I will let it go, but remember I will be counting his cuddles. Mummy Cathy and daddy Kevin also had their adoption meeting today. It went on for well over an hour. They should be really good parents now, after that. Daddy Kevin opened a bottle of coke and made a noise. People looked round at him. He was sooo embarrassed. It didn't help that by the time they had left Percy and got top the adoption education centre they were a minute or 2 late. The teacher was waiting at the door for them. They were lucky not to get lines or detention. There was no room at the tables for them so that had to sit in the naughty corner. I am feeling happy now, daddy Kevin just gave me a sneaky jam tart. I had the blackcurrant one and he had the strawberry one. I had finished mine before him and still managed to drool for his. It worked< I got a little piece. Yummy. Percy is going in for his surgery hopefully on

Monday if the vet says he is well enough. I hope he is. We all want him to come home. Get well Percius. Night night.......

Well I was taken to meet my new brother today. I was so nervous in the car travelling to Evesham. When we arrived mummy Cathy went to the office to let them know we had arrived. Daddy Kevin started walking me to the paddock where we were to walk together. Percy came towards me with a handler and mummy Cathy. Immediately he was growling at me. I went to say hello and sniff him. He went to bite my ear. His name Tyson suits him well. I said to him, I am not Evander Holyfield. We were kept apart and brought together again. This time he got me. He nicked the end of my tongue. He caught me off guard. There was blood pouring from my mouth. Mummy Cathy was starting to panic. She came to hug me and check my injury. It was decided that Tyson/Percy didn't like me and wasn't going to change his mind. He was taken back to his kennel. He had blown his chance of coming home with us. I know it is sad, but I haven't been brought up to fight and I couldn't fight my way out of a paper bag. I thought for a minute they had taken me to self defence classes. Peace man!!!! Mummy Cathy is now looking at adopting another boxer. He is tan and white and a bigger scaredy cat than me. He lived in a nasty place and was used as a stud dog. He never saw people to play with and so is scared of people. He is tiny. Only a third of my size. He is a really pretty dog. His name is Mitch, (at the moment). This will be a long adoption because of his nerves. Mummy and daddy are busy tonight looking after their little wounded soldier. I am traumatised. I will have night mares tonight. I also have a scratch down my face from Tyson. Why didn't he like me? I am so loveable. It is sad because Tyson will struggle to find a new home if he carries on being spiteful. I am going to rest now as it has been a long stressful day. ....

Hello. I have been very quiet this week. Mummy Cathy has been poorly. Massive headache she couldn't get rid of. I almost had a sister but that will keep for another day. Grrrr. I am too traumatised to think about this right now. Mummy Cathy and daddy Kevin have decided to just keep me on my own. They say I am too spoilt to have a brother or sister. What does spoilt mean? I am kind. You can share my food and water if you want too. I only share your things because you force me too. The sky man was meant to come today to install new phone line and internet. Whoops he didn't come. Mummy Cathy went mental on the phone at the sky man. He said he had run out of time to come to our house. Mummy Cathy asked if would self combust if he had stayed out late. Daddy Kevin had sat waiting all afternoon for nothing. He was not happy. Mummy Cathy has promised to take me to the park tomorrow as she has not seen much of me this week. Soooo looking forward to this. I must remember to be good!! My nephew Joey went to Weston the other day with his school. He went to the sea life centre. I like fishes. Especially one from the chippy shop. Yummy. Joey also did Prince of Wales training. What is this? Did he train to be a Prince? Will I have to bow as I is a bow wow. Joey is also running in the relay race. He is sooo fast. He is bound to win. It is Daddy's day after 2 more big sleeps. I cannot wait. This must involve sweets and a big dinner. It is Sunday as well which means roast dinner. This is my favourite dinner. Mmmmmm. I wonder if daddy Kevin is as excited as I am. Mummy Cathy has got the fan on in the lounge. I is shivering. Does she think it is summer time. Night night. I shall dream of something warm.......

Hey its daddys day tomorrow. I am so excited. Lots of food and also I get to my sis Michelle. Mummy Cathy was poorly again this morning with her headache. She is ok now though. Mummy Cathy has been busy making soup and a meringue for tomorrow. She is making something called Eton mess. Messy or not I will eat it. Mmm. I went to the park today. I only ran off once. I went swimming in the pond. Mummy Cathy was so proud.

Carrying on. I might get a length certificate for my swimming. I will have problems wearing jim jams to dive for brick though. Where will mummy Cathy sew my badges? So many things to worry about. Mummy Cathy is going to a car boot sale again tomorrow. What does she want a car boot for? Almost as bad as daddy Kevin going swimming Pool with no towel. He also went to see Gym today. Who is Gym. Night night time .....

Happy Fathers day to my lovely daddy Kevin. Thank you for all my walkies and treats. I promise to try and and be a good boy from now on!!! What times dinner? What do you mean I have to go to sleep first!!!

Happy father's day to Alan knight. You are the best daddy Lauren, Shannon, Joseph and Eleanor could have. xxxxxxxxxxxxxxxxx

This is a special message from Michelle Fraser. You are a very special person. Whom we absolutely love to bits and adore. The message sent to Kevin was beautiful. It is not often Kevin is speechless but he was and had a tear in his eyes.

A massive thank you to Michelle, Alan and our Beautiful grandchildren. xxxxx

Wow it is still father's day. Really it is. I have eaten so much, I was actually sick. Because I do not chew my food there were whole chunks of meat and a potato. I have said it wasn't because I was a pig it was because I had my worming tablets and they always make me sick. My brother Michael came and had some dinner. Mummy Cathy and daddy Kevin had almost finished theirs when he came in. He had his dinner, played with me, chatted a little bit and was gone. Michael says he is watching football on telly. Boring or what!!!! It is funny how people say mummy Cathy threw Michael out. Surely if she did this then he wouldn't visit her so often and have meals with us. He cannot survive without mummy Cathy's Sunday roast. Daddy Kevin had some lovely cards today. My sis Michelle and Alan gave him a lovely card which had lovely words inside. Shannon, Joseph and Eleanor made daddy Kevin a fabulous card, which he loved. Of course I gave him a card with one of my brilliant pieces of poetry inside. Mummy Cathy also gave him a card. I thought it was his birthday for a minute and then I remembered. Silly me. Mummy Cathy and Michelle and Shannon went to a car boot sale earlier. They didn't buy any car boots though. Maybe the right colour wasn't for sale. Mummy Cathy did by Michael a big china old pub ash tray. Mummy Cathy said to look after it because they are not made any more. They are now plastic. There were some big china pigs for sale. Mummy Cathy and Michelle both liked them. One was £4 and the other was £3. They ummed and ahhed and walked away. They went back later and the middle sized £3 piggy had gone. The lady (a trader) still had the £4 piggy for sale. Again they ummed and ahhed and went to walk away. The lady then produced a small piggy for £1. Where from, they didn't know. Mummy Cathy bought it for Michelle. Daddy Kevin came to pick them up. He had been practicing his golf. Remember the walking and hitting a little ball around with a stick. Odd game. Anyway he said he was starving and sent mummy Cathy to get him a burger. She came back with a dried up, over cooked cheese burger. £4.50. Mummy Cathy said she could have bought the pig for that and Michelle said and had 50p change. Lol. After all the fun and food today I am feeling tired. I shall say nite nite now. Is it daddy's day boxing day tomorrow? Mummy Cathy has just said that I am just being silly. Me being silly, does she listen to herself? Night night ....

Well that's another day over. I told you I was poorly yesterday because mummy Cathy made me take nasty tablets. My lovely dinner I had all came back. Weirdly it looked exactly the same as when it was in my bowl. Mummy Cathy says it is because I never chew my food. Mummy Cathy went to bed last night, (she had to get up before daddy Kevin to go to work) and left me with daddy Kevin. It then became his job to clear up after me. 1.30 In the morning and then I had an empty belly. Guess what, I was starving. I went to my food dish for a bit of a late night snack. I would have preferred chocolate but daddy Kevin wasn't offering. Daddy Kevin has still got a chocolate orange from Christmas. He probably has an Easter egg or two as well. Daddy Kevin really loves chocolate but he forgets to eat it and buys more. He is sooo silly. Mummy Cathy was so pleased when she got home from work today. I had only been on my own for about one and a half hours. Daddy Kevin is on late's and he goes at 4pm and mummy Cathy gets in at half 5. As I said mummy Cathy was really happy when she came home tonight. Daddy Kevin had text her to say he had cooked her tea and it was in the oven for her. How good is that? What he didn't tell her was that he hadn't done the washing up. Mummy Cathy opened the front door, I was there waiting with my yellow baby. (Yellow baby is my favourite), she went into the kitchen and was greeted with a side full of washing up. Not only that but as I have said I had only been on my own for an hour. I had had 3 big pee's on kitchen floor. Welcome home mummy Cathy. I was jumping around her with my yellow baby. She was trying to give me cuddles whilst assessing the mess from both me and daddy Kevin. Daddy Kevin text (after she had moaned at him) to say, leave washing up and he would do it but too late, she doesn't hang around it had already been done. I think for a little while we were both in the dog house. Whoops. Mummy Cathy doesn't stay cross for long though. She has washed up, cleared up, made the sandwiches for tomorrow and cooked daddy Kevin some sausage rolls for work. I wanted them but so far I haven't managed to have them. Grrr. Mummy Cathy bought a bicycle seat cover today. Don't know why. She hasn't even got a bike. Lol. It is for my sis Michelle. To stop her getting a wet bottom when she rides to work. My sis would beat Bradley Wiggins in a race and that Stretch Armstrong bloke. Anyways I am yawning now so I say night night. ....

I have had a quiet day today. Work was boring. Bed testing has lost its attraction. I might have to look for another job. I am not sure what though as for most things I am probably over qualified. I fancy the idea of a chocolate taster for either Cadbury or Thornton's. Or an ice-cream taster for walls. Magnums all day long. Are they made by walls? I was thinking, maybe join the police as a police dog. Then I remembered a telly programme I watched with daddy Kevin. This Alsatian dog had to jump over walls, without knowing what was on the other side. Chase after all kinds of knobheads. Really putting his life in danger. Do you know what treat he got at the end of that, a bonio, a chewy stick, a sausage roll? Nooooo all he got was a manky old tennis ball. And it wasn't even a new one. I don't think I am cut out for the police. I am not very fond of tennis balls. What about a sniffer dog. I could work at the airport sniffing out drugs in people's luggage. I might find all kind of goodies. mmmmmm. Hang on though, what if I accidently sniffed something up my nose. I could become an addict. Mummy Cathy would put me in doggy rehab. I would have to find a human and beg outside marks and spencers, or sell the big issue in the cold and rain. Brrrrr. Okay forget being a sniffer dog. I wonder if Greggs are looking for new staff. I would be brilliant in there. I could taste the food, tidy it away (in my tummy). If I worked in Greggs I could pop round to my sister's house on my lunch break. We could have a cup of tea and a fondant ring dough-nut together. Yummmmmmmm. I am going to have some very nice dreams tonight. If you have any good ideas for my future employment please tell me as I would be very interested. Nothing too energetic mind as I am getting old now!!!! Night night ....

As my new job. Maybe I could be daddy Kevin's security guard. I could go to the pool and watch daddy Kevin do swimming with his big stick, or visiting Gym with his bag. I could even go to work with him and guard his food bag. I would love to do this. Only when he is on late shift. No early mornings for me. I need my beauty sleep!!!!! Only one small problem with this though. I would probably find away into his bag and borrow his lunch. Not sure he would want it back though. Please Please daddy Kevin, Can I!!!!!!!!

What a nasty, stuffy, muggy day it has been today. Bed testing is difficult when the weather is sticky because it is too hot to lie down. I would like to be a penguin when the weather is hot and skate around on the ice. Not sure about the skating part though. Mummy Cathy is not happy with sky. Last week they were meant to come and didn't. Today they came, unannounced. Spent two hours connecting broadband and phone. Phone doesn't work and broadband is still virgin's as sky's isn't working. She has just blasted them an email. I am glad it wasn't sent to me. Mummy Cathy has been very busy since she came home from work today. It was grampy Dennis's birthday last week while they were on holiday. Mummy Cathy and daddy Kevin didn't know what to buy him as a gift. They have decided that mummy Cathy would make him a birthday cake. It smells yummy. MMMMMM. Mummy Cathy didn't make a cake for my birthday. Grrrr. I will remember for my next birthday!!! I scared the life out of mummy Cathy last night. You know how they say children and animals can see spirits around the home. My niece Eleanor saw one a couple of months ago. She was playing at the kitchen table when she looked up and smiled. Mummy Cathy asked who she was looking at and she replied the lady. It was only Mummy Cathy, Eleanor and me in the house. Strange. Well last night mummy Cathy went up to bed about 11.45pm. Daddy Kevin was at work. I always go up the stairs with her and check she is in bed safe and sound then I normally go downstairs to one of my many beds. Well last night I led at the top of the stairs looking at something in the hall way. Mummy Cathy heard a cry of some sort and came out to see if I was okay. She didn't expect me to still be on the landing. My eyes were wide open and I was looking as someone was downstairs and mummy Cathy was sure she could hear the television. Even though she had turned it off. All of a sudden I went running down the stairs excited as if daddy Kevin was home but there was no-one home. I then went to bed and well, mummy Cathy was awake half the night having nightmares. I quite often stare up the stairs as if I can see someone. Strange!!! Mummy Cathy wants a peaceful night tonight. I am tired now so I say night night. Sleep tight. Hope I haven't scared you..... BOO!!!!!

Wow, have you seen the birthday cake mummy Cathy has made for grampy Dennis. It has taken her hours. Coconut, almonds, icing and marzipan and lots of different colour food colourings. She must have the patience of a saint. Mummy Cathy really didn't expect it to turn out as well as it did. Daddy Kevin didn't either. Mummy Cathy is shattered now. I sat there patiently waiting to see if she would drop bits on the floor for me but she didn't. At one point, I actually got shut out of the kitchen, can you believe that. Mummy Cathy thought I might steal the cake. As if I would. What have I ever stolen? Okay, I admit I stole the bread she made and had left on the side for one minute. The occasional sandwich daddy Kevin has left on the table, but apart from that nothing at all. Sometimes I think they just over react. When mummy Cathy had finished and all the washing up was done she gave me a sweet from the side. Thank you mummy Cathy. I have stayed up way past my bed time today because mummy Cathy has been busy. In the evening I do not like to be in the lounge on my own. I am not scared or anything. Well maybe a little bit. Mummy Cathy is sitting down to watch television for half hour now before she goes to bed. I think I might curl up on the other sofa and tuck my toes in now. This means go to sleep in case you didn't understand. Night night........ mmmm I am dreaming of cake already.....

What a strange day we have had today!!!! Mummy Cathy woke up at 7.30am with a migraine. She came down stairs and took some pain killers. While she was up she put all of daddy Kevin's work clothes out to dry on the washing line. She then went back to bed to shift her migraine. She heard knocking on the front door. It was my brother Michael. Swaying in the wind like a bendy flower. He was very very very drunk. He said he had come "home" to use the loo as he needed a wee. He hasn't lived at home since January. He had a pee and then went to sleep in his old room as if it was still his room. Mummy Cathy unfolded the guest bed which is normally only used by the lovely Shannon and Eleanor. Mummy Cathy put a blanket over Michael and off to sleep he went. Mummy Cathy went back to bed and spent the next 30 minutes vomiting. She then went back to sleep. Mummy Cathy stayed in bed until lunchtime and then got up to start the Sunday roast. Michael came downstairs looking worried. Have I emptied my pockets he asked? He hadn't. He had no door keys with him, no cigarettes and no i-fone. What the hell he had been doing in the night he didn't know. Mummy Cathy thinks he got so drunk that in his head the flat was his friends and not his. He then decided to walk home. We took him back to his flat, passing his friend who had stayed the night driving home. Michael pressed the entrance buzzer to his flats. No-one would let him in. Let's hope he hasn't upset them all. Luckily for us a man was coming home and let us in. We went to Mike's flat and yes it was unlocked. His keys and ciggie were there but no phone. We searched everywhere but nothing. We left Mike in his flat so that he could sober up properly. Mummy Cathy and daddy Kevin went home and started to ring Mike's mobile. No luck, it was ringing but with no reply. Nothing more to be done for now. I went into garden with Daddy Kevin; he was cleaning his golf sticks. He must be going for a walk with the little ball soon. I think he takes the sticks for company. He had a bowl of soapy water with him in the garden. It was ever so windy today, all of a sudden the bubbles flew across the garden trying to attack me. Where could I go, I couldn't even get past them. Again and again they tried to get me. I became so scared that I poohed myself 3 times. How embarrassing!!! I then found my old chicken toy. It is all tatty and chewed up but I love it. Anyway mummy Cathy is still cooking dinner after all the trials and tribulations of the day. She again tried to call Mike's phone. A man answered. He had found the phone in the high street earlier in the morning and was now in Maiden Head. The i-fone has gone on holiday for a few days. Probably needed a break from Michael. Lol. The man says he is back in Cheltenham on Tuesday and made arrangements for the collection of the phone. Mummy Cathy and daddy Kevin have been back to Mike's to let him know. He is better now. Mummy Cathy has given him a dinner to warm up. She said she will make him a badge with his name and address on in case he gets lost again. She said he is a dinlow!!!! Because mummy Cathy and daddy Kevin have been running around seeing to Mike. I haven't even had a walkies today or nothing. Grrrr. After all this going on I have started to feel really sleepy..........

Well I am back online again tonight. Mummy Cathy had another Migraine yesterday. She came in from work went straight to the bathroom. She was then sick and I didn't see her again. She went to bed with her migraine. Why is the migraine allowed on the bed but I am not? It was a sad day for her at her work office today as a lady called Lynne was leaving. Mummy Cathy likes this lady a lot. Lynne has helped her with pc stuff. Mummy Cathy isn't very techie at all. She needs all of the help she can get. Lynne has also given mummy Cathy hugs when she has been upset. A big hug and a thank you Lynne from me!!!!! Remember the other day when my brother Michael got very very very drunk and left his flat to come to our house for a pee. What a dough-nut. Remember his phone upped and left him and went on a short break to Maidenhead. It is back now. I hope it had a good time and took lots of pics. I hope Michael learns to appreciate it or it might run away for longer next time!!!! Mummy Cathy's phone has gone back to Virgin (not a virgin) to be repaired. This is the 2nd time in 3 months. Mummy Cathy is always arguing with Virgin. Daddy Kevin is going out in a minute. He is not going swimming tonight with his stick. He is watching other people in the pool with their sticks. I wonder if they have towels. I will have to try and remember to ask daddy Kevin when he gets back. Daddy Kevin went to see gym yesterday with his big bag. Still haven't met gym. Daddy Kevin also went for a walk with his big back of sticks and white balls yesterday. He said he was doing some driving out on the range. Home home on the range, where the deer and the antelope play. That's all I know of that song. I think it is out of an old musical called Oklahoma. Mummy Cathy says I am daft. Hang on who is writing this? It is time for m e to hang up my spurs and get some shut eye. I am getting the hang of this cowboy (dog) stuff. Maybe daddy Kevin will take me out on the range with him................

Well it's been a few days since I have been on f/b. Hope I have been missed. Mummy Cathy has been on late shift this week and when she gets home she is too tired (and grumpy) to type for me. I shall have to train up daddy Kevin. That's if he is not too busy with Gym, or swimming with sticks and oh yes, chasing white balls with more sticks. Daddy Kevin is a busssssssy man. Lol. Do you remember the story last weekend of my brother Michael and is run away phone. Mummy Cathy saw Michael last night and he bit her head off. All she asked was had Mike taken the name and number of the chap that returned phone. Mike said he had. (mm not sure) Mummy Cathy asked if she could have it to call and thank him personally as she was the person who spoke with him on Sunday. Mike told her in no uncertain terms that it was his business and nothing to do with her and that he would do it. This was Thursday evening and he got the phone back on Tuesday morning. Why hadn't he rang the chap then? Michael doesn't see that he should say thank you. His attitude was the chap couldn't use it and so had to give it back. Wrong, he could have just binned it or smashed it up. The thoughtful man didn't have to do anything with the phone. SOOOOO anyway a massive thank you to kind chap. Next time though do me a favour and put it in nearest bin!!!! Before this, mummy Cathy had offered to go to Mike's flat and give it a clean and tidy and pop all of his washing to the launderette. (This was before the phone saga) Blimey, red rag to a bull. Mummy Cathy just thought as he isn't used to doing proper house work. Cleaning your bedroom once in a blue moon isn't the same. He might appreciate a hand from her. I think if Michael had had a gun he would have shot her. He must have been in a foul mood last night because he really took it out on mummy Cathy. I don't know what it is about my 2 brothers. I don't know why they cannot just be nice. Mummy Cathy had only gone to meet daddy Kevin at his swimming pool (with sticks) on her way home from work. Mummy Cathy was glad to get home. Mummy Cathy will not go to swimming with sticks again. Please feel sorry for me now!!!! I was poorly on Wednesday night. All night. I sometimes do this thing. I am in a trance, I cannot hear anyone or really see anyone. I keep licking things. The air, floor walls furniture, anything at all. This normally goes on for about 5 hours. During this time I am very very sick and everywhere. It is disgusting for daddy Kevin and mummy Cathy to clear up. It isn't very nice for them to see me like it either. I only have this about 4 times a year though. On Thursday, I was so tired from lack of sleep and being sick the night before. I was feeling very sorry for myself. Mummy Cathy and daddy Kevin just gave me cuddles. Mummy Cathy hoovered and then steamed the floors with disinfectant. Mummy Cathy has the rug out in the garden (from the lounge), I was sick all over the rug. She is going to scrub it tomorrow when she gets in from work. Sorrrrreeeee mummy Cathy. Mummy Cathy is just glad I am better. I was naughty yesterday morning. When daddy Kevin got up at 5am and went to work, I crept upstairs and somehow without waking mummy Cathy I went to sleep on their big bed. It is sooooo soft and comfy. It would have been worth a telling off for being on it, I didn't get told off though. I am reallllly spoilt. I am going to end now as I am getting a sore throat from saying all of these words to mummy Cathy...............

What a night I have had. Mummy Cathy has just watched last week's Waterloo road. She thought Grantly was going to die. She was sobbing like a baby, I had to jump on her lap and give her a cuddle. She was so upset. She will be going to work tomorrow with swollen eyes. Mummy Cathy woke me up with her crying earlier. She watched last night's Paul O'Grady, For the love of dogs done at Battersea dogs home. There was a puppy so mis-treated. It broke mummy Cathy's heart and she sobbed like a baby at this also. All in all she has cried all night. I think mummy Cathy uses these programmes to cry about all sorts in her life. I thing the sad bits in films etc are just triggers. She seems to have settled down now so I am going back to sleep. Night night.......

I have just heard about a bunch of old men who have gone away playing golf. That walking game with sticks and little balls. Well apparently the old, old men all got drunk as skunks. (Wilf and Colin) lol. Hope heads okay this morning. Go on old gits show the youngsters how to do it.Haha.

What a strange day it has been. Mummy Cathy had to get up early to go to work. I was too sleepy to say bye to her. I had just woken up when she came home. I am not a morning person (dog). Mummy Cathy hasn't stopped since she came in. She has washed and dried and put away all washing. Cleaned the house from top to bottom. She also scrubbed the rug. She struggled with that because it is so big and heavy. You are probably not meant to scrub it with washing powder and a scrubbing brush but it looks as good as new now. It is over the swing seat drying. It will probably be there for a week. LOL. Mummy Cathy gave me a piggy leg for being a good boy. You should have seen the mess I made with it. Sorreeee mummy Cathy, but you did give it to me. Mummy Cathy is hoping for a sunny day tomorrow so that she can sit in the garden and enjoy it. Daddy Kevin sent some photo's of his golf place. It is just grass and nothing else. No other dogs or people or nothing. What would I do there? The grass looked very green though. It wouldn't look like that after I had peed on it and run across a few times. It must be really boring watching a little ball rolling on grass. Maybe if I was there I could fetch the ball and take it back to daddy Kevin. He wouldn't have to follow it then. The only problem with this would be, I am not very good at returning things. I could learn though. I am tired now though, it's all that watching mummy Cathy rushing around today.Yawn..........

Mummy Cathy has just been sat in garden topping up her tan with a cold bottle of lager and a bowl of strawberries and cream. It is finally summer time (for the weekend anyway)

Hey one more big sleep and daddy Kevin will be home. I do miss him when he is not here. Mummy Cathy has looked after me though so I am okay. Truth is she spoils me rotten. Mummy Cathy was speaking to Nanny Brenda on the phone earlier. Nanny Brenda was changing channels on her telly last night when she accidentally pressed the standby button and turned telly off. She then didn't know how to switch it back on. She had to phone her brother to come round today to do it for her. I don't mean to laugh but on/off it is not rocket science. Sorry Nanny Brenda. You really do need to become more independent. Mummy Cathy says, you let women kind down depending on men all of the time. We have had another beautiful day today. In Devon it has been cloudy. Mummy Cathy has just been cross with me. She scrubbed the rug in the garden yesterday because I was sick on it. She has only just got it dry and put back in lounge. Whoops one of my spots has been bleeding all on clean rug. Mummy Cathy has had to clean it again. Sorrrreee. Mummy Cathy is having a chicken sandwich for her tea. I hope she remembers that I like chicken also!!! Mummy Cathy was chatting on phone with my sister Michelle earlier about people who try to ruin other people's lives with spite and evil. These people really cannot be happy. If they were truly happy they wouldn't have time for anything else. On that note I am going to look for the chicken sandwich, well the chicken really. ....

I have just heard about a bunch of old men who have gone away playing golf. That walking game with sticks and little balls. Well apparently the old, old men all got drunk as skunks. (Wilf and Colin) lol. Hope heads okay this morning. Go on old gits show the youngsters how to do it.Haha.

Mummy Cathy has just told me a story about grampy Dennis on her and daddy Kevin's wedding day. Grampy Dennis isn't much of a drinker except for the odd tumbler of southern comfort. During the reception there was free red/ white wine, as much as anyone wanted really. As I have said Grampy Dennis doesn't drink very often but took a liking to the red wine. He drank getting on about 2-3 bottles. After the reception he went to bed to sleep it off and almost missed the whole of the evening do Nanny Brenda was furious with him. His head must have had a brass band playing in it. Fair play, he carried on for an hour smiling and laughing but he didn't have another drink. Daddy Kevin has just rang mummy Cathy and told her they had free wine on their tables at dinner tonight. Friday and Saturday night Grampy Dennis hasn't bought a drink, free wine on the table and he had 3 big glasses. Daddy Kevin has said he is very merry. I hope he has some paracetamol with him for his head tomorrow. At least he hasn't got Nanny Brenda there to nag him for it. Grampy Dennis, you have a good night. We all love you.........X

I have just heard about a bunch of old men who have gone away playing golf. That walking game with sticks and little balls. Well apparently the old, old men all got drunk as skunks. (Wilf and Colin) lol. Hope heads okay this morning. Go on old gits show the youngsters how to do it.Haha.

Mummy Cathy has just heard from daddy Kevin, They are on their way home. There is now a golf geek's convoy heading towards the M5. I am just getting ready to have a nap before daddy Kevin comes home so that I will be as fresh as a daisy and full of energy. I wonder if he has bought us a pressie. Nahhhhh. He never has before when he has gone on the old man's golf tour. Mummy Cathy is doing him a special tea tonight. Daddy Kevin has been having 3 course meals for the last 3 days. Haha, back to normal for him now. Michelle, stop eating them sweets, they will rot your teeth!!! Lol. Good luck to Shannon and her mum Michelle. They have their 1st visit to Shannon's secondary school this evening. The school will seem huge to Shannon after primary. Anyways, nap time

Daddy Kevin has just emailed to say they were at services on the M5. They seem to be taking an awful long time driving home. Maybe they have run out of petrol and are being pushed. Come on old men, foot down, you are allowed to touch 70mph. I will have to have another nap at this rate.....

Well guess what. Daddy Kevin is home. He didn't bring me or mummy Cathy a pressie from his trip. Not even a stick of rock. What a meanie. It's a good job mummy Cathy is thoughtful. She filled my Kong toy (a hollow bouncy kind of toy with a smallish whole at one end) with soft cheese and peanut butter with some of my doggy bikkys inside. It is doggy heaven. You keep licking until the bikkys fall out. MMMMMMMM. Daddy Kevin has gone for a shower now. It didn't seem overly happy to be home. I suppose it is back to work for him tomorrow. Still he should be happy he has had a few days away. Mummy Cathy has been here working like a cart horse. Mummy Cathy is feeling a bit sad. I hope all the other golfing geeks haven't gone home to their wives grumpy. daddy Kevin stopped at services on way home and bought 2 small bottles of Pepsi and a small bar of galaxy and guess how much. Over £5. They saw him coming. Mummy Cathy has got to carry on doing tea now and then put daddy Kevin's washing on. Maybe he will smile when he has his tea........

Daddy Kevin is in a better mood now. I think he has been mixing with too many grumpy old men and came home behaving like one. He read my last message and has said sorry for being a misery. I think he has had a brilliant time as he hasn't shut up about it yet. (Boring). Daddy Kevin is creeping round mummy Cathy now. I do not like it when then kiss and cuddle, Yucky. I am the one to give slobbery kisses!!!! Daddy Kevin has been playing ball with me in the garden that was until mummy Cathy took her flip flop off. Remember the slipper/flip flop game. It doesn't matter what the time is, the game still works. I was just too slow this time, mummy Cathy quickly put the flip flop back on. What I hadn't seen was daddy Kevin rolls my ball to the other side of the garden. By the time I realized I was going frantic. I really thought I had lost my ball. I was so relieved when I found it. Phew!!! I went and sat on the swing seat then with Daddy Kevin. Now daddy

Kevin knows I do not like to swing too much on it. It gives me tummy ache. Daddy Kevin kept swinging it, I couldn't get comfortable and then my leg fell off down the back of the seat. I was sooooo embarrassed, why did they have to laugh at me. I had to go and hide in the corner and hide my humiliation. Mummy Cathy said sorry and gave me a big cuddle. I am okay now, I have both mummy Cathy and daddy Kevin home together. All is well in the world. Night night............

Everything is back to normal in the Haysome house. Mummy Cathy gets up and goes to work. Daddy Kevin stays in bed. Daddy kevin goes to work and then mummy Cathy comes home. Mummy Cathy does stuff and spoils me, then she goes to bed. It is almost time then for daddy kevin to come home and go to bed. This is how my week goes. I am lucky really as I am not on my own very much. It is hard to do my bed testing job sometimes though with all of the comings and goings. I have just been frightend. Mummy Cathy has this dog thing in the lounge by the fire. It is always watching me. Scarey it is. I dropped my kong toy which then hit the fireside tool set. Clang clang clang it went. It always makes me jump. Mummy Cathy said it is like the Monday 9.30 fire alarm test where she works. Anyway my kong toy hit the fireside tools and then hit the dog. I swear he growled at me. The problem was a biscuit fell out of my kong toy. I had to get it before he did. I slowly shuffled over and grabbed it but I could hear the other dog growling at me. He was saying Grrrrr Grrrr at me. Do you know what , it was mummy Cathy. How could she be so mean to me. I was being so brave aswell. I am still scared of dog though even if mummy Cathy says he isn't real. Daddy Kevin took me for a lovely walk today . It was great to be me and daddy together again. Mummy Cathy cannot take me for walks because I am to strong for her. It is not because I am naughty, I am just excitable.Mummy Cathy has just cooked some sausage rolls for daddy Kevin for work. She has also done some in case he has the munchies when he comes home. I hope he does so we can share. I will have to try to remember to wake up when he come home. On that note, night night.......

Mummy Cathy has said she is just tooooo tired to be helping me with my story tonight. She has come in from work and then spent 30mins on phone moaning too sky. The person then hung up on her. How rude. Mummy Cathy wasn't being rude or anything, just explaining things. She then sent them yet another email which they won't reply too. She then spent 45 mins on phone to virgin regarding her phone and the train wreck that is virgin. Pardon her language but mummy Cathy said they are really taking the piss. On the plus side mummy Cathy's mobile came back from being repaired today, on the minus side daddy Kevin was in the shower and so didn't answer the door so it is now sleeping the night at the post office. I am trying to keep out of her way as her mood isn't the best!!!! I must be getting old. There is a big buzzy fly in window of lounge and I cannot catch it. I was going to have it for my pudding but will have to go without. I can hear it buzzzing. Buzz buzz buzz. Grrrr. Mummy Cathy is doing daddy Kevin lunch for tomorrow now, he has got fish. Mummy Cathy told him he would have to sort it himself but she is such a softy. When mummy Cathy came home tonight I gave her my Kong toy to be filled with treats again but she said no. mummy Cathy said I cannot have sweets every day. I don't know why. Last month at the vet, they said I was perfect. They cannot be wrong can they? Grrr. I spent all day working on the beds dreaming of my sweets. Never mind grrr maybe tomorrow. Mummy Cathy has set their sky box to record something about starlings. Why, she knows I am frightened of them. Remember the bullyish starling last year that attacked me in my own garden. I am still traumatised by it. Everything seems to attack me. Mummy Cathy has a fireside set by the fire and the shovel thing jumped of its stand and nearly hit me once. Another time in the garden by the shed daddy Kevin had a spade stood up. I was minding my own business playing with my ball and yep you have guessed it, that also jumped out on me and hit me on my head. I still will not go by the side of the shed because I know that the spade is waiting for me. Don't get me started about Tyson (Percy) who was going to be my new brother. I still bear the scars from him. I never do anyone any harm. Everything is out to get me or so it seems. That starling though was really mean; he nearly had my eyes out. Why is she recording starlings? AAAh she says it is not about birdies, so all is well... Mummy Cathy says I am daft, I so am not. Anyway mummy Cathy must be as mad as a box of frogs. She is the one typing a story about me and my antics. LOL. Sorry mummy Cathy , we all know I tell you what too write really.... night night....

Hey guess what!!! Mummy Cathy's phone came back today. Before we all start singing and dancing for joy. They sent it back as it was. Not mended, not even looked at. They sent a letter with it saying she had sent the wrong blackberry. Mummy Cathy only has 1 backberry!!! She has been on the phone from 5.30pm when she got home from work until 7.20pm. She has still got nowhere. It is a good job there isn't a virgin shop in Cheltenham anymore as I think she would murder someone. Almost 2 weeks without her phone and they still expect bill to be paid. Really!!! Theyu arein for a shock. I bet they will contact mummy Cathy quick enough then!!!....

Mummy Cathy sends a big thank you for the box of cherries daddy Kevin bought her today, they have become her tea.....

Troy we are sat in a bar in Spain and Roger wants to know what you've been doing today roger been sun bathing and in the pool now having a pint of San Miguel. This is a message I received today from My Auntie and Uncle. What a nosey pair. Lol

I am a little bit later today because mummy Cathy and Daddy Kevin have just been food shopping. When they go food shopping it is normally daylight and daddy Kevin comes home smelling of sausages and with egg round his mouth. Apparently they go to a burger van. This isn't a van made out of burgers, although that does sound yummy. Daddy Kevin always has an egg and sausage bap. Mummy Cathy has egg and bacon and sometimes (usually) brings me home some bacon wrapped in foil. I am gutted. No foil packages tonight. Nothing for me at all. I even greeted them with my Kong toy, which I am still waiting to have filled with treats. Last night when mummy Cathy was watching telly. Allegedly I was snoring very loudly. I couldn't hear it and not sure I believe it. Well she was watching a dog programme about sad dogs needing homes. All of a sudden she burst out laughing. I almost jumped out of my fur. I ran out of the room with fright. I sneaked back in when I knew it was safe. Mummy Cathy did give me a cuddle and said she was sorry. When mummy Cathy got up for work this morning, it was my turn to give her a shock. My legs and bedtime duvet were covered in blood. There were spots of blood on the floor. It looked like I had been attacked. Mummy Cathy nearly missed her bus because she was checking me over to see where I had been bleeding from. Mummy Cathy couldn't find anything wrong with me and no more bleeding. Very odd. Daddy Kevin thinks it was just one of my teenage spots bursting. Sorry if you are eating!!!. Mummy Cathy has been lazy tonight. She came home from work, waited for the virgin mobile man to call back at 6pm. Obviously he didn't. Mummy Cathy then went to bed for an hour. She got up just before daddy Kevin came home from work. I almost forgot to say. When mummy Cathy came home from work she sat in the garden in the sunshine for a bit. Well you all know I do not like birds. Especially starlings. Well a big fat pigeon landed in the garden. It must have been thirsty because the only puddle in the garden was the one I had peed, and it was drinking from the puddle. Yuck or what. They truly are vermin with wings. What is worse the second part of our back garden where there is a gate to stop me going in there. This is because I am partial to munching on pebbles. They are nicer than they look. Anyway in the 2nd part of the garden, mummy Cathy has put a bowl of water, some bread and a couple of cherries for these flying vermin. What did I get? A pat on the head. I think I am the loser here. I am being dragged out now for a walk. It is dark and scary. I do not like the dark. Too many shadows jump out on me. I am a proper scaredy cat. It is worse for daddy Kevin as he cannot see the cats hiding. Ha-ha, I always see them. I am not scared of them! Anyway until tomorrow...

You may think it is not stressful. After nearly bleeding to death. I still had to stay at home and work at bed testing. It is not all fun and games for me you know. I don't know how I did it really. I was feeling pretty weak... Thank fully i didn't need a transfusion and am well again now.....

A special hello to my favourite auntie and uncle who are busy having fun in the sun. Daddy Kevin got up at the crack of dawn this morning (7.30am). He woke me up and made me go out for a pee pee. Now anyone that knows me knows that I am not a morning person (dog). I like to wake up in my own time and saunter outside in private. When I came in I could hear mummy Cathy calling me. She was singing the morning song to me. Now the morning song is brilliant, I wriggle and wag my tail as mummy sings her song to me. The song goes, a morning to you, a morning to you, a morning mummies woofuls , a morning to you. Then repeat. Then it goes. A morning, a morning, do be do a morning, a morning a morning to you. You need to hear it to truly love it like I do. I do not think mummy Cathy would sing it to anyone else though! Anyway as I was saying, mummy Cathy was up as well. This is unheard of unless she is going to work. The next thing they are putting food into a bag and saying bye to me. What is going on? Oh I get it, they have decided to go out for the day and leave me on my own. I might have to ring social services or child line at this rate. It is not fair, I didn't get to share any of the food!!! All they left me was my dog food and a bowl of water. Anybody would think I was just any old dog. I am a pedigree you know. Any way they came back this afternoon. Daddy Kevin has gone a funny pink colour. Mummy Cathy keeps laughing at him. Mummy Cathy says she did warn him he was going pink. Whoops daddy Kevin is not happy. Lol. They drove down to Weston and mummy Cathy has say in a deck chair and not moved. Daddy Kevin went to a pub to watch 2nd half of rugby. Well done to the lions. I didn't know lions played rugby. Do tigers and panthers play also? I know the bears in Chicago play games. When mummy Cathy and daddy Kevin were walking to the beach after parking the car. They passed a female beach volley ball game being set up. Daddy Kevin mentioned something about it. Mummy Cathy said NO they were not watching it. Poor daddy Kevin. When he said he was watching the rugby, maybe he went to watch volleyball. Mummy Cathy has just cooked beef stir fry in a garlic and black bean sauce for tea. I have been sat dribbling. It smelt yummy. There was also garlic dough balls. I am having to give my best guilt trip looks. It works every time. Ha-ha suckers.......

I am so excited. Mummy Cathy has filled my Kong toy up for me. It has strawberry jam (sugar free), I have to watch my weight. Peanut butter, marmalade and soft cheese. Last but not least my doggy treats. It is in the freezer now. This is so that it will last me longer. Daddy Kevin is going to take a pic of it later to show you all what my Kong toy is. Daddy Kevin is out in the front garden painting the front gate. It has been on his to do list since 2001. Not too long then. Lol. He will be getting third degree burns out in the heat today. Auntie Sue and Uncle Roger, I hope you are watching the tennis with a pint...

Mummy Cathy didn't read before she typed today for me so I didn't know you were coming home today. Glad you home safe and sound. Mummy Cathy and daddy Kevin would love to go with you. They don't think twice about leaving me behind. Tell Uncle Roger to behave and stop looking at the girlies. Lol. Enjoy tea and tennis. Gooooo Andy!!!!!

What a scorcher today. Can't believe mummy Cathy still cooked her Sunday roast. She says it is not Sunday without one. Daddy Kevin filled up a massive drinking bowl for me today. Daddy Kevin calls it a paddling pool. Why would I want to paddle in it? Water is for drinking, not playing in. Do you know what was really rude? Daddy Kevin sat in a chair in the garden and then put his feet in my new drinking bowl (paddling pool). Disgusting, I have to drink this water. Mummy Cathy is in the dog house. Why do we say dog house. Everyone knows dogs don't have houses. I am spoilt but even I don't have my own des res. Anyway, mummy Cathy has been naughty. She has phoned Nanny Brenda. There was no one home and so Mummy Cathy left a message mentioning the fabulous tennis and Andy Murray winning. Apparently daddy Kevin has said that Nanny Brenda and grampy Dennis will have recorded it to watch later. This means that if she picks message up mummy Cathy will have spoilt the surprise for them. Mummy Cathy has said they should have stayed home and watched it live as it was a brilliant game. It was too hot to play golf anyway!!! Sorreeeee nanny and grampy. I was helping daddy Kevin sweeping in the garden this afternoon. I don't know what it is with garden implements but the broom jumped and tried to attack me. I am not helping any more. Daddy Kevin has given me my Kong toy now. It is soooo cold. MMMMMMMMMMMMMMMMMM. Lovely. That big fat pigeon I was telling you about yesterday. Well it has come into the garden about 10 times today. I don't know why. Daddy Kevin said, it is just teasing me. It sits on the floor for as long as it can and flies just at the last minute. I am getting cross now. It is my garden and doesn't belong to any pigeons. Mummy Cathy says it reminds her of the pigeon in a programme Michelle used to watch when she was young. Pigeon Street. I cannot imagine a programme about pigeons in a street. Was it like Coronation Street or Brookside? I guess it wasn't very popular as it not on any more. Anyway I am bust eating my Kong now. I would share with my auntie Sue and Uncle Roger but they are not here. You do not know what you are missing!!!!!!

I have got to be busy now. Mummy Cathy has been approached by a publisher to publish my stories. OMG we are all going to be famous. Auntie Sue, who do you want to play you on the silver screen? Everybody thought Marley was cute, wait until they meet me!!!!It will be Pudsey who. Hahaha. Mummy Cathy has still got issues with her mobile. Virgin have still not mended it. She has not had her blackberry for 3 weeks now. She has had strawberries though and last weekend, I saw her eating cherries. Mummy Cathy hasn't heard from Nanny Brenda yet, with message on Sunday so I guess she hasn't picked up the message. Uncle Roger, I bet it feels like Spain with this heat when sat with a cold drink in garden? I got told off tonight by daddy Kevin. Meanie. It was so hot last night when mummy Cathy and daddy Kevin went to bed, so I followed them up the stairs. They have got air conditioning in their bedroom. Mummy Cathy normally isn't allowed to use it as daddy Kevin moans at her and says he is cold. Anyway at the moment with this mini heat wave mummy Cathy is allowed to use it. I jumped onto the bed and led in the middle with my legs on my side of the bed. Daddy Kevin seems to think this is his side of the bed. I don't know why he thinks this. When daddy Kevin was away with the old men with sticks and balls. Mummy Cathy told me this was my side of the bed. Last night just as I was getting comfy, he kept shoving me and pushed me off. How rude is that. I had to come back downstairs and sleep on the floor where it was cool. I will get arther itus from sleeping on stone floors. Daddy Kevin if you are reading this I hope you are feeling guilty especially after telling me off when I finished my shift at bed testing today. Mummy Cathy has been talking with my sister Michelle tonight on the phone and Michelle is excited about my pages maybe being printed. A book, a film, premieres and red carpets. soooo exciting. Daddy Kevin, stop being mean to me. Whose side of the bed is it? Poor little Joey is poorly. Too much sun, we are just not used to it. Mummy Cathy cooled me off with the hose pipe tonight. I didn't like it at first but it was lovely and cool. Daddy Kevin sat in deck chair sunning himself. He is well jel of mummy Cathy's sun tan. He says he is catching up. Lol. It is time for me to go sleep now. Daddy Kevin is out at the pool again. He has got his stick thing with him. No towel though. Not so bad in this weather as he will dry really quickly. I have to be asleep before daddy Kevin comes in or he might ground me for laughing about him. Night night. Get well soon Joey....XXXXX

Message for my lovely sister Michelle. Peggy is coming back into Eastenders. Just for one single episode. Ronnie is coming back to help Roxy with her wedding to Alfie, and Phil is going to be shed loads of trouble. Peggy is coming to sort em all out. She will shout, Get aaaat my boooooozer the lorr of ya.

Hey, I have just remembered something daddy Kevin said to me yesterday. I was minding my own business in the garden. I was taking a cool drink of water from my new big bowl. Daddy Kevin shouted at me, Stop drinking the water. I am putting my feet in that. What a cheek. Daddy Kevin

I think it is time for me to share the story of Dixie with you. I was so traumatised at the time, I didn't want to think about her. Remember when mummy Cathy and daddy Kevin were thinking of adopting another child (dog). First they introduced me to the most savage of savages, Tyson. They should have been alerted by the name alone. I still do not know why he didn't like me. I am beautiful and a joy to be around. I am a gentle giant. I still have the scars from my meeting with Tyson. Well next they decided that maybe a puppy was the way to go. They brought home a tiny little puppy. They christened her Dixie and she was 9 weeks old. She was introduced to me and immediately I went to sniff her and she cuddled into my mummy Cathy. My mummy Cathy not her mummy Cathy!!!. I was put into my room so that they could show Dixie around the house. Her new home. As soon as they put her down she was running everywhere. Daddy Kevin decided he would take me out for a walk and a chat. Father to son sort of thing. Meanwhile Dixie is getting all comfy with my mummy Cathy. I was not happy, but I was going to have to accept it as Dixie wasn't going anywhere. When we got home from our father and son chat/walk, the horror story began. The tiny thing that was Dixie came at me like a banshee. Barking and snarling. I was petrified. I am no fighter. I never ever bark. Well only when I want to go out for a pee or to have my water bowl refilled. Mummy Cathy picked Dixie up and took her to the spare room with her food and water. I had a cuddle to calm my nerves. The next day mummy Cathy decided to let us play together. Dixie was very crafty and sly. She would run under the sofa and then try and get me when I went looking for her. What had they brought home? She was a she devil in disguise as a cuddly puppy. Now mummy Cathy and daddy Kevin both know I am afraid of small things that bark. When I was about 5 months old and quite big in size. I was coming home from a walk with mummy Cathy and my brother Jonathan. We were almost home. Out of nowhere came a man and a yappy little white dog. This dog kept barking at me. I led on the path and wet myself with fright. I was so scared my legs went to jelly and I had to be dragged home as I couldn't walk. All this with Dixie went on for a few days. I wasn't eating, I wasn't sleeping. It was a true nightmare. I was thinking of packing up my toys and running away. I couldn't even do that, hop would I have crossed the roads without daddy Kevin to help me. In the end mummy Cathy and daddy Kevin decided to find a new family for Dixie. They found a mummy and daddy and 2 little girls. She went to live in Cirencester in a lovely house with a big garden. Mummy Cathy was sad to see her go but knew it was for the best. As for me, I won't fib about it. I was glad to see the back of her. At last I had my house back and my mummy Cathy and daddy Kevin all to myself. It has been decided that there will be no other pets in our house. I am the only one. Now you can understand why I couldn't speak of this before. I still have nightmares about her!!!!

This is a message for daddy Kevin. When I was on face book earlier today. I wasn't skiving as you thought I was. I was on my tea break. I don't know why it is a tea break when all I get is water. Sometimes I am spoilt and I am given milk. This is only when mummy Cathy and daddy Kevin think the milk is going off. Oh yes it is alright to give me a belly ache with sour milk. Anyway, so I was on my break. I hope you wasn't being naughty using your phone when you should have been working, daddy Kevin!!! I was playing in the garden earlier and you should have heard the foul language. Why is it foul language? It isn't chicken language. I thought there was some Irish navvies working in next doors garden. Sorry Irish navvies, it is just a phrase. Anyway it wasn't, it was just the young girl and her friend. They were ffing and jeffinng as I said like Irish navvies. Sorry again Irish navvies. This girl is only about 10 years old. Mummy Cathy said she would wash her mouth out with soap and water. I shall ask my sister Michelle about that one. Mummy Cathy told me to come in, she doesn't want me picking up language like that!!! I am going to settle down now as I am plum tuckered out (tired). Daddy Kevin has just dragged me out for a walk. Mummy Cathy has written a formal complaint to Virgin. Written, by hand with a pen, how old fashioned is that!! Mummy Cathy asked daddy Kevin to post the letter. He decided to find the post box furthest away. I am soooo tired and my legs ache. night night, any chance of a massage.......

Hello. I am a poorly boy today. I have been up all night again being sick. Daddy Kevin got up this morning to a right mess from me. Daddy Kevin is so kind sometimes. He didn't moan or anything. It was 5am in the morning and he was getting ready for work. He gave me a cuddle and sorted me out best he could. Thank you daddy Kevin. When mummy Cathy got up I was still feeling poorly. Mummy Cathy has also given me a cuddle. Mummy Cathy has filled my water bowl again before she went to work and tucked me into bed. I am allowed a sick day from work. I think I may have sunstroke and exhaustion. I work far tooooo hard! I am going to rest now as mummy Cathy says sleep is nature's medicine. Thank you mummy Cathy and daddy Kevin.

Hey you know what they say. You can't keep a good man (dog) down. Thank you for all the get well wishes today. I m feeling lots better. My ribs feel as if they are broken and my throat is sore from being sick and retching. I have even managed a little bit of my food but that hurts to swallow.

Mummy Cathy is thinking of letting me have a weetabix with some warm milk. Poor mummy Cathy, when she came home from work she had to hoover all downstairs and the landing and then steam the floors all downstairs and the landing carpet from where I was sick last night. Daddy Kevin was kind though, he did get the hoover out of the cupboard for her ready for when she came in. Sooooo kind. Mind you, it was daddy Kevin that cleared the sick up at 5am today. I have taken it steady today. I have just napped and rested. I wonder if I will have to work tomorrow.

I might see if I can have another day off. After all I really am poorly. I can't believe daddy Kevin sometimes. Here I am on my sickbed and he has gone off to the pool. Mummy Cathy said to him where is your stick? Daddy Kevin said he had left it in a cupboard. A cupboard in a pool. Would that be a locker? Daddy Kevin said he had to go to the pool because there was only going to be four of them. Mummy Cathy thinks he would be lovely in a pool with only four people in it. I still don't understand why they have sticks. Weirder still, why do they have the blue chalk? Daddy Kevin was going to play the walking game with more sticks tomorrow with grampy Dennis but he can't now as he is working overtime. How can you work over time? You cannot see time. Daddy Kevin does say and do some funny things. He has been on the phone to Nanny Brenda trying to sort this walking stick thing out. Daddy Kevin says it is really hard work. Nanny Brenda and grampy Dennis both talk together and then to daddy Kevin and nobody listens to anybody. Mummy Cathy laughs a lot whilst this is going on. Daddy Kevin did a funny hand gesture to mummy Cathy. It was like a wave but with only 2 fingers. This made mummy Cathy laugh even more. Daddy Kevin still doesn't know if the stick game is tomorrow tea time or on Saturday morning. It is soooo confusing. Mummy Cathy has just watered the vegetables in the garden. Mummy Cathy calls it her plantation. She has carrots, cabbages, curly kale, broad beans, runner beans and French beans. I nearly forgot the corn on the cob, tomatoes and lots of rhubarb. Mummy Cathy is a proper Alan Titchmarch. I don't like carrots, they are horrible. If mummy Cathy puts carrots in my dinner, I always manage to find them and spit them on the floor. Yuck. Sometimes they get mashed and I eat them without realizing. That is crafty of mummy Cathy. Meat is my favourite but daddy Kevin says we cannot grow that. Although mummy Cathy did want a pig once. Daddy Kevin almost let her have one, only almost though. Mummy Cathy and daddy Kevin went on a day out to Adams farm, (the farmer from country file). They had piglets there for sale only £20. What a bargain. I would have loved it. A real edible toy. I have only had piggy ears, trotters and a snout before. I have just remembered, I have had the crackling part before. All this talk of food is making me hungry. I wonder if I can have my weetabix before bedtime. I shall go and see.......

It is time to tell you all about me and my family. Daddy Kevin has said I should have done this already. Sorreeeeeeeeee. My name is Troy. I am a 6 year old white male boxer. I am quite a large boy, and weigh around seven and a half stone. (45kg) I am not fat though, I am solid muscle. Mummy Cathy says I have love handles around my hips when I sit down. Also mummy Cathy laughs at my back feet. The skin rolls down by my ankles looking like a pair of fallen down socks. It's rude to laugh mummy Cathy. You are no Twiggy yourself. When I was born I lived with my birth mummy with my brothers and sisters. We were all sent when we were about 8 weeks old to live with new mummies in new families. Even then I was quite a chunky boy. Everybody knew I was never going to be small. I was 3 months old and my new parents didn't want me. How could they not want me? I was gorgeous. I was pure white all over except for what looked like eyeliner under one eye. I have also got the blackest eyes you have ever seen. Soooooo cute!!!. I was taken back to my birth mother. I wasn't wanted. Because I am a white boxer I am deemed worthless. What a cheek. Mummy Cathy and daddy Kevin had just lost their little dog Mickey. They were grieving and not looking for another dog. A friend of daddy Kevin's had a white boxer and both mummy Cathy and daddy Kevin had both said they would maybe like one in the future. Mummy Cathy happened to hear my sad story from a lady called Sue Brown. This was a lady mummy Cathy used to work with. It was arranged for me to come to meet my new parents. I was soooo nervous. Would they like me, would they want me? I bounded around their garden, all legs and ears flying everywhere. Daddy Kevin couldn't believe the size of me for a puppy. I was staying, they loved me. I would never replace Mickey but I now had new parents. I didn't know it then but I was about to become the luckiest dog ever. No-one could ever love me more than my new mummy and daddy. Meet mummy Cathy and daddy Kevin. Daddy Kevin works really hard. He works as a machine operative, welding car parts for a large car company. His hobbies are obviously me, swimming (getting wet), going to see Gym (he is mysterious), playing with a pool (not swimming) and a stick, walking with sticks and following a ball (Golf). Daddy Kevin has a lot of hobbies. He also watches a lot of sport on a big black rectangle on the wall. Football, rugby, golf, anything really!!! Mummy Cathy works in an office. She is a debt collector. Mummy Cathy says she loves her job and the people she works with are fun. Her hobbies are again obviously me and anything to do with me. She also enjoys cooking and using daddy Kevin as a guinea pig to try new recipes. She doesn't really have many hobbies as she is also kept busy with house work. Mummy Cathy says she doesn't have time to go gallivanting around like daddy Kevin. I also have a big sister named Michelle. She spoils me also. Michelle gets me a massive bag of bones from her local butcher. MMMMM, thank you Michelle. She doesn't live very far from us so I get to walk to her house sometimes. Michelle works hard, she cares for the elderly. Michelle has a partner called Alan. He is a very quiet person and I think very shy. He is a fantastic dad to their children. Alan also grows a lot of vegetables in their garden. Now there are four gorgeous children, my nieces and nephew. Lauren who is 13. Lauren lives with her dad at the moment. She is just going through her troubled teens. She is a lucky girl to have 2 families that love her. Michelle misses her a great deal as do her siblings. Next is Shannon. Shannon who is gorgeous 11 years old. She is getting ready to go to senior high school in September. Soooo grown up. She is a really good swimmer and not afraid to try different strokes. Daddy Kevin taught her how to do the butterfly stroke. Now onto Joseph. He is a proper rough and tumble boy. He has a really cheeky face. He is really good at athletics. Maybe an Olympian in the future. He used to be really afraid of me because he had previously experienced nasty dogs. Not nice friendly dogs like me. We are cool together now. Last but not least is Eleanor. What can I say about this little madam? I have never known anything with as much energy as Eleanor. Also she eats more than I do. That is saying something. She is as bright as a button and afraid of nothing. There is also a rabbit that lives in the garden.

He doesn't talk; he just stares and twitches his nose. I bet he would taste nice with gravy, yummy. I must remember to ask Michelle. Well I have to mention grrrr a kitty cat called Penny. Grrrr. She is cute and pretty enough but she is still a cat. Grrrrr. Cats are the enemy. I do not know why they are the enemy but they are. This is my sister's family.

Next is my brother Jonathan. He lives with his girlfriend Sarah. They have a little boy who is almost 2 called Dylan. He is a little cutie. Jonathan also has a little girl called Isabelle. She is 3 now and lives with her mum Kayleigh. We haven't seen Isabella since she was a baby. Jonathan fell out with Kayleigh and he has moved on with his new family now. Isabella if you read this in the future we all love you. Sarah is now having a little girl also. Mummy Cathy and daddy Kevin do not see Jonathan and Sarah. I know they miss seeing Dylan growing up. Jonathan was mean to both mummy Cathy and daddy Kevin so for now they are apart. I think it is probably for the best. My other brother is Michael. He also doesn't live with me. He has a flat in town and takes care of himself. He gets drunk a lot so is better living on his own. Michael visits lots and has Sunday dinners with us. This always means less for me as he always has seconds. Piggy Michael. Well that is the family and how I came to live with them. I will carry on with my daily stories of life in the Haysome house hold. If I find out who Gym is I will let you know or if you know him pleeeeeease tell me!!!!!!!

This is a message from mummy Cathy. I have beat the ***holes that go by the company name of Virgin mobile. I emailed them again yesterday and no reply. Rang them yesterday evening. They said they would cancel my contract but set up a new one with a new handset. I agreed to this. A lady called Irma cancelled contract and was setting up new contract with a new Samsung. She said she was having problems setting up and so she said she would call me back in 30 minutes. I think I have heard this before. After waiting an hour, I again called. The poor lad I next spoke to started getting cocky with me. I told him to drop the attitude and read notes. This time they had no excuses and I left them with no argument to come back at me. I had given them the rope and yep they have hung themselves. My contract ended 8 months early and I have got an email confirming. Off to get new phone on a different network soon. The moral is, if you are right, stick to your guns and do not back down...

Me and mummy Cathy have been busy today. Not daddy Kevin though. He has gone with grampy Dennis walking with sticks. I cannot understand why they chase the little balls. Some of the little balls do try to escape into little holes but they never manage it, they are always found. There are others though who are cleverer they hide in long grass and are never found, and others (the ones that can swim) hide in ponds. These are the clever ones. Me and mummy Cathy have been doing house work. Mummy Cathy has also picked from the plantation some broad beans and some curly kale for tomorrow's dinner. Yes in this heat mummy Cathy will still cook a Sunday roast. She has dried lots and lots of washing in the sunshine. The best thing is mummy Cathy has made me some doggy ice-lollies. She bought come 15p chicken stock cubes in Tesco. She dissolved them in hot water and then added in cold water. She then poured into her silicone muffin moulds and froze them I have just had one and yummy. I think I had brain freeze. Brrrrrr. Ha-ha daddy Kevin you haven't got one. Mummy Cathy is having a nice cold glass of cider now before we go to scrub the toilet. As for me I am now led in the shade to have forty winks...

Mummy Cathy has just had a major accident in the kitchen and what a stink. She was moving something in a cupboard and I heard an almighty smash. I came running of course to see what it was, (it may have been edible), and she had knocked over a bottle of vinegar. Glass was all over the floor along with the vinegar. She had to spend half an hour sweeping, mopping and steaming floor to clean it up. Don't tell her I was giggling, she will be cross with me. Good job daddy Kevin was at work or she would have blamed him. When mummy Cathy came home from work I met her with my black baby. He was still on the kitchen floor. Mummy Cathy has thrown him into the garden now as he was

in the middle of the vinegar pool. Poor black baby. I am happy again now as I have the rug back in lunge. Mummy Cathy had to hoover and scrub it again yesterday as I was sick on it again. Mummy Cathy says it is becoming a habit. Remember my friend Eric. I think I must have upset him, I can't think what I could have done but I haven't seen him for a few days. I hope he hasn't met a new friend and broken friends with me. I shall ignore him when he does visit again. Mummy Cathy has cooked daddy Kevin half a chicken tonight to go with salad before he goes to work tomorrow. I hope she remembers to tell him he has to share!!! Do you know what happened to me this morning? It was terrible! Mummy Cathy came downstairs to go to work. As I was awake I thought I will go into the garden. Normally she gives me a treat to get me to come in. I totally forgot daddy Kevin was still home and she could leave the back door open. I sat there, and sat there for ages. When I came in she had gone. No mummy Cathy and no treat. How bad is that!!! She didn't even kiss me bye bye. Mummy Cathy said sorry when she came home and told me she was in a hurry as she had over slept. Serves her right! I had a drink out of my big water bowl yesterday and you will never guess what was in it. There was tadpoles from a froggy. Does that mean I will pee out frogs? Yuck. Daddy Kevin has cleaned it out now and refilled it for me. Daddy Kevin has put some tadpoles in a jar for Joey. They are funny little wiggly things. Joey, do not drink them though!!! Daddy Kevin bought some boogie boards today. That sounds disgusting. Ohhhh, mummy Cathy says they are boogie boards for going in the sea on. They are going to the seaside soon with Michelle and the girls. I do not like the sea or the sand. The sand gets all in my willy and it really gets sore. Mummy Cathy had to clean it with a bottle of water. She gets all of the good jobs. Ha-ha. Sorry mummy Cathy but you took me there. Daddy Kevin kept dragging me into the sea. He wanted to see if I could swim. He is silly, he knows I have never had lessons. I didn't even have a rubber ring or leg bands or anything. I could have sunk like a stone!!! I much prefer grass. I am going to sleep now and dream about running like the wind.....

What a treat I have had tonight. Mummy Cathy did my Kong toy again for me. Peanut butter with cheese spread and some chunks of cheese in as well. MMMMMMMMMMMMMM, Scrumptious. Thank you mummy Cathy. You are lucky to still hear from me today. Daddy Kevin is on late's this week and is also working overtime so gets home at early hours of the morning. As I was up and about and it was cool out at this time daddy Kevin decided to take me for a walk. Well we were just strolling along, chatting, man talk when daddy Kevin noticed we were being followed. It was more like stalking. We have all watched those David Attenborough programme's. The ones where he is in a warm studio with a parka on pretending he is at the South Pole or somewhere. Mummy Cathy says, she doesn't even think he has a passport. He is just added in for affect when programme is finished. Anyway back to last night. We was being stalked by a wild animal. Daddy Kevin says it was a fox but it was more like a mountain lion. I could see its teeth and everything. You could tell it was crouching down ready to pounce. My heart was in my mouth, I can tell you. Even daddy Kevin must have been scared because we had to run home. I was so scared I wanted daddy Kevin to pick me up and carry me but he wouldn't. He said it's every man (dog) for himself. I am so scared it is hiding in next doors tree waiting to pounce on me. After all, he could live on me for a week and still have some left for the freezer. That's if he has a freezer. Wild life is meant to be on the telly, not in Hester's Way. It is bad enough when mummy Cathy tells the ghost stories of Hester in Hester's way and Maud the witch of Maud's Elm. I hope daddy Kevin doesn't want to go hunting again tonight. I am Troy not Mowgli daddy Kevin. I am going to finish eating the contents of my Kong toy and then it is time for sleepys. I hope I don't have nightmares.....

Firstly a message from mummy Cathy. We have heard Kevin's dad Dennis has prostate cancer. He is a strong active and generally healthy man. I cannot think of a kinder, loving father and grandfather than Dennis. I am sure everyone that knows and loves him as we do will join me in saying, Dennis you can beat this. We will be with all of the way with whatever you need from us. All of our love and prayers are with you and Brenda.XXX

OOOH I had one of my ice lollies again tonight when mummy Cathy came home from work. I was looking all hot and bothered. What she didn't realize was that I was testing a lovely soft sofa this afternoon and well you can guess. Yep I had a good afternoon sleep on it. I have now put a passed inspection label on the sofa. My job is ssoooo difficult!!!! Daddy Kevin dragged me for another walk in the middle of the night. The birds were tweeting and the sun was coming up. Daddy Kevin thought it was lovely. Me I couldn't see, I think I was sleep walking. Mummy Cathy sleep walks and talks in her sleep. A few weeks ago, daddy Kevin thinks she is a nut job. She got her makeup out and plastered it all over the bed. Worst part was when she washed it on a 90 degree wash it wouldn't come out. Daddy Kevin has said she has ruined it. Another time she searched through a cupboard to get the mosquito repellent and placed it on her dressing table. Normally she just walks to the loo for a pee. It frightens daddy Kevin as he thinks she is going to fall down the stairs. My sister Michelle also used to sleep walk. She used to walk around the house putting all of the lights on. Mummy Cathy used to wake and follow her and turn them off again and make sure she went back to bed. The worse time was when she had a high cabin bed with a wardrobe underneath. She went smack straight to the floor. She didn't even have a bruise the next day. Lucky girl. Anyway back to my walk. We didn't meet David Attenborough or any wild animals. It was just a peaceful cool walk. I imagine that mountain lion (fox) was looking for us last night but we fooled him by going at 4 instead of 3. Ha-ha Gotcha. I have had to eat my own dinner tonight as mummy

Cathy only had weetabix. Boring. She has done meatballs in a spicy sauce for daddy Kevin. I won't be allowed that either as it will burn my bottom on the way back out. Mummy Cathy won't want me having a baddie belly when she gets on from work. I shall have to think about napping again in a minute. I imagine daddy Kevin will be dragging me out again. There are never any cats out at this time. You would think this would be the best time to get the birdies as they would be all bleary eyed. I still haven't seen Eric. Mummy Cathy thought she saw him but she couldn't be sure. Mummy Cathy says he will be back when he has finished sulking!!! Well I won't lose any sleep over Eric. It is his loss. Most pigeon would be grateful to have a friend like me to play with......

OOOH before I go to sleep I have got to share this with you. Mummy Cathy has just made daddy Kevin's sandwiches for tomorrow. He has got smokey chicken with spicy wholegrain mustard. Mummy Cathy as I have already said has done him meat balls in a spicy sauce with pasta. I have just had chicken, with 2 meatballs and some pasta. No sauce though for reasons I have already explained. It was yummy! Now daddy Kevin what did I used to do when I was really happy. Let me remind you. I had a bush in the corner of the garden, not in anyone's way, doing no harm at all. I loved that bush and mummy Cathy called it my special bush. When I was young I chewed up every plant shrub and tree in the garden until all that was left was my special bush. I used to love rubbing my back on it. It used to make me feel so happy. Well one day when mummy Cathy came home from work she found daddy Kevin in the back garden. He had been weeding or something. Anyways she looked at my special bush and screamed OMG what have you done to Troycies special bush. Daddy Kevin had decided to give it a hair cut (prune it). All that was left was one branch, nothing else. I was devastated. I sobbed like a baby. Before I knew it the whole thing was dug up. This was a year or two ago and do you know what I did tonight. I went over to my special bush, I forgot it wasn't there. There are so many disappointments in life. I will never forget my bush. I hope you are sorry daddy Kevin!!! I did get my own back though. Daddy Kevin had a recliner deck check in the garden with a padded seat. For days and days I pee'd on that chair. He had to get rid of it in the end. Ha-ha. Revenge was mine.....

There are some people who are saying mummy Cathy is some sort of a weirdo pretending to be a dog. Let me say, if this offends you, then do not read it!!! Also these pages are not about mummy Cathy. She is not pretending to be a dog. I am a dog. A pure bred pedigree boxer dog. These stories are just life through my eyes told my mummy Cathy. Anyways. It has been so hot today. My day started as normal which a marathon walk with daddy Kevin at 4am this morning. I am beginning to look forward to our man talks and walks. We discuss everything. At the moment we are discussing the golf. Why these men are paid so much money to walk around with their sticks chasing the little white balls. If fox hunting has been banned (they still out there looking for me) then little ball hunting should be also. Maybe I should contact David Cameron and see what he says. Our other topic is Wayne Rooney. Chelsea or not. We think yes. We do not think he will be staying at Man u any longer. Man u have had some good years from him but time to let him go while they can still get good money from him. A free transfer in a couple of years is worth nothing. He didn't have a brilliant season last year, like he has in the past so let the sulky scouser gooo. Now daddy

Kevin has said there are cats out when we are walking but he doesn't let me see them. Well let me tell you daddy Kevin. I will be alert tonight. Ears and eyes everywhere. I willllll find them if they are there! MMMM I have just had some cheese chunks from mummy Cathy and then had to clean my teeth ready for bed. I am up late tonight because it is sooo hot. Plus it is harder to get to sleep when like me you nap in the daytime. I really should try to stay awake more. It is difficult to test comfy beds without dropping off. Almost like a perk of the job. Anyways mummy Cathy says I have to go to sleep now ready for my walk as daddy Kevin will be home earlier tonight. Night night......

I was so disappointed when mummy Cathy came home from work. No offence to mummy Cathy but you don't bring food home like daddy Kevin. I don't know why I thought they would be together. I must have been having a blonde moment. Daddy Kevin takes lots of food to work because he has been working 12 hour shifts this week and usually he eats it all. This week though, because it has been so hot he has been bringing some home. I have done quite well I can tell you. Anyway when mummy Cathy came in, I fetched my Kong toy and went looking for daddy Kevin. Mummy Cathy said he will be home in a big minute. This means an hour. I looked out of the window, no sight of him. A few minutes ago , when I wasn't looking for him, he came home. He had to ring the door bell because mummy Cathy had left her keys in the door. Silly mummy Cathy. Daddy Kevin is in a bad mood with mummy Cathy. Mummy Cathy used to be a smoker but she quit almost 3 years ago. Mummy Cathy has been a bit stressed this week and bought some cigarettes. Daddy Kevin is like inspector Morse (grumpy) and found the cigarettes. Daddy Kevin, what was you doing in mummy Cathy's bag anyway? You are naughty too. Daddy Kevin is still in a bad mood. Mummy Cathy has left him sat in the garden to sulk on his own. He will get over it she has said. But just for the record she has stopped smoking again now daddy Kevin. I was poorly again in the night. I am always sick in the night. I do not know why. Daddy Kevin cleared it up when he came home. I am ok now though, I think it is just the hot nights. It is sooo hard to sleep. There was a spider in our bathroom the other night, I knew there was something I had forgotten to share with you all. I think David Attenborough brought it round because he didn't like what mummy Cathy said about him. This was a massive spider and I mean massive. You knew he was tough. He had a shaved head, puffa jacket and doc martin boots on. Now sorry to all of you insect lovers. Yuck. Mummy Cathy was petrified. The only thing she could think of to get it was hairspray. After spraying him she flattened it with her slipper. I am sure I heard him say I'LL BE BACK! Any way daddy Kevin is taking me out for a walk now........I still haven't seen Eric. If anybody does see him. You can't miss him. He is big and fat. Tell him to sod off!!!

Mummy Cathy and daddy Kevin took Michelle, Shannon and Eleanor to Weston for the day. Thank heavens they took sun cream. Mummy Cathy said it was very hot and sunny. Mummy Cathy paddled in the sea with Eleanor. Daddy Kevin built sand castles with Eleanor. Poor Shannon is 11 now and mummy Cathy says she is at a difficult age. She is not little any more and not a teen yet. She was bored at everything. Mummy Cathy and my sis Michelle couldn't please her with anything. Mummy Cathy is contacting Weston super mare council to ask if they will remove the sand from the beach for Shannon.

No more sand castles. Both girls rode on donkeys. We tried to get Michelle to go on one but they said she was too old. She is the same size as a 12 year old!! The donkeys only went about 10 feet. A rip off for £2. Amazing how many stupid people let babies lie out in sun on blankets. No shade or anything. Just stupid!!! I have just had some treats. Bits of pizza, some ham, and bits of a roll. Yummy. I like it when there are left over's. I hope Alan, Mike and Joseph had a brilliant time at Fairford Air show. How can you have a show about air? You cannot see air. Strange. I am now going to lie in shade in garden and look for Eric. Eric where are you.....

What a horrible 24 hours I have had. I was poorly again last night. It was my funny licking thing. I was so sick and I was up all night with it. You have never seen mess like it. I was still poorly today when mummy Cathy went to work. She gave me a cuddle and filled my water bowl and off she went. No thought for the baby she was leaving behind. Mummy Cathy was also mean to Shannon yesterday. Mummy Cathy and daddy Kevin took Shannon to the fair. There were only 2 rides left open, everything else was for babies. Shannon went on the sizzler with daddy Kevin and loved it. Mummy Cathy persuaded her to go on the other ride. Mummy Cathy doesn't go on rides as she is a scaredy cat and so doesn't realize how horrible some of them are. Mummy Cathy says they are all horrible. OMG, this ride when spinning one way then the other and then upside down. If mummy Cathy could have turned it off she would have done. Shannon, mummy Cathy is sooo sorry. She will make it up to you. I will make sure. Shannon was so poorly. Shannon won some nice teddies though and she beat mummy Cathy at darts! My brother Alan and his brother Mike were cooking a barbecue last night. Mike asked

Eleanor to put some hot sauce on a burger. Well she put some on (loads), Mike's mouth was on fire, and he could barely talk. But fair play he didn't waste the burger. Lol. I am waiting for mummy Cathy to finish cooking dinner. She had a hospital appointment this afternoon and so was late home. Excuses excuses. Mummy Cathy get that dinner cooked!! I am just resting after my ordeal. My chest hurts and my throat is sore. I might need to go to the vet as this is the 3rd time I have had my licky sickness in 3 weeks. Normally I only have it 2-3 times a year. I really do look poorly I am not just trying to get time off work. Although I did have a day off today. Daddy Kevin thinks I may be allergic to something so they are going to be careful now with what I have. OHHH oh, I hope this doesn't mean diet time again.....

Daddy Kevin has just posted some pics on face book. There is Mike with Joey and Eleanor on his shoulders. This was after the burger burnt his mouth and throat and stomach. After this they played hurdles, jumping over garden chairs. Those kids are Olympians of the future!!! Mike Knight will be their trainer. Mummy Cathy and daddy Kevin had their dinner and because I have been poorly. I got nothing. Mummy Cathy then ate an ice-lolly and she didn't save me anything. Greedy gutz, mummy Cathy!!! Daddy Kevin has also posted some pics of me with a toad in my mouth. When it rains we get lots of toads in our garden. I don't know why? We haven't got a pond. They jump about when they think I am not looking. Ha-ha, too slow. Gotcha. It takes mummy Cathy and daddy Kevin ages to get them off me. I rarely hurt them. I just hold them in my mouth. I don't know why. It isn't because they taste nice either. Mummy Cathy has too rinse my mouth out after as when I have finally released them back into the wild, my mouth starts pouring with saliva. Mummy Cathy says the whole thing is disgusting. I do pretty much the same with slugs and snails. Mummy Cathy doesn't like them either. Lol. I hope that David Attenborough chap isn't going to come and tell me off. I don't mean to do it. I have said before, I am not naughty I am mischievous....

Mummy Cathy is home from work and busy doing stuff ready for tomorrow. Meals, sarnies etc. Nothing for me. Mummy Cathy did give me one of my treats. I sneaked upstairs with it to eat it on the big comfy bed but the door was shut. That wasn't fair. I ate it on the landing. Sorry mummy Cathy in advance before you goes upstairs if I have made a mess. Oops. I had such fun this morning. Mummy Cathy is on lates so she doesn't have to get up so early. I was bored of waiting for her to appear and as Daddy Kevin had left the door open I sneaked in like a commando on my belly. Mummy Cathy didn't see or hear me come in. Oooh I am good at this commando stuff. Maybe I could be an army dog or a police dog. Would I have to work away from home do you think? I wouldn't want that. I would miss my home comforts too much. The dogs that are in the army and police are very brave though!! Anyway. I sneaked into the bedroom and jumped on the bed and threw myself onto mummy Cathy. I was led right across her neck and face. I could hear spluttering noises. I think she was singing the morning song to me although it sounded like choking! I will have to tell her her singing voice isn't what it was. Lol. Mummy Cathy eventually freed herself from under my grip. I was wagging my tail so fast I almost took off like a helicopter. I jumped off the bed quickly before she could shove me off but then jumped back on. Boing boing, sooo much fun. I then ran around the bedroom and played hide and seek with mummy Cathy's slipper. Quick time to go I thought. Mummy Cathy has the slipper back now though. I wonder where she will hide it tonight for me? Mummy Cathy has just taken some chicken pieces out of the freezer for tomorrow. Mmmmm I do like chicken. I will have to guard the fridge tonight. I do not want that mountain lion from last week coming in (he knows where I live) and stealing it. If there is stealing to be done it is to be done by me. Daddy Kevin is out tonight gallivanting with his stick. He has gone to the pool again with it. What does he do with a stick in a pool? Answers on a postcard please. Only kidding. What is a postcard anyhow? Daddy Kevin hasn't been to see gym lately. Maybe they have fallen out like Eric and me. Mummy Cathy saw Eric at the weekend but he didn't speak. I am going to grab some zzzz's now before I go on guard duty........

Congratulations to Jackie. I hear you are to join the nanny club. Lovely news. Really happy for you all. X

A massive HAPPY BIRTHDAY to Joseph who is 8 today. From nanny and grampy and Troycie XXXXXXXX

Have fun at sleep over. Sleep tight; don't let the bed bugs bite. LOl

I have been very quiet over the last few days. We have all been working hard and due to the heat have been very tired. Mummy Cathy has been on late shift this week so I have lost my typist. Mummy Cathy come on pull your finger out, this diary will not write itself!! It was Joseph's birthday yesterday and he was 8. Mummy Cathy made him a spider cake. It looked yummy. I didn't get to eat it though. I was hoping she would drop in on the floor but no such luck. Grrrr. I have hard at work this week practising the slipper game. Mummy Cathy will have to buy new ones soon as we are wearing the ones we use for the game out. It is mummy Cathy's fault though because in between our games she wears them. Mummy Cathy stop it. When mummy Cathy was walking home from work last night she could see in the distance the mountain lion. No sign of Sir David though or his camera team. The mountain lion (fox) saw mummy Cathy and went to hide behind a hedge. Mummy Cathy was carrying home McDonald for her tea. (Lazy mummy Cathy). She was sure the lion would smell the food and chase her. Mummy Cathy is such a baby. Everybody knows that the lions like to catch their own food and cook. I know they like fast food, like zebras etc. I don't think you are likely to catch a mountain lion or a fox queuing up in KFC. They have more sense!!! Daddy Kevin went out with his stick to the pool last night. Mummy Cathy popped into see him on her way home from work but they had hidden the pool. There was just lots of men stood around leaning on their sticks. We are now none the wiser. You let us down mummy Cathy!!! Today Daddy Kevin, grampy Dennis and Nanny Brenda have gone hunting white balls. I hope they manage to get away. Run little balls into the long grass or into the pond. Daddy Kevin has gone off with his big hunting bag with more sticks in and a food parcel. Daddy Kevin means business today!! Anyway, no rest for the wicked. Some of us have to get back to work....

Ha-ha. Such fun this morning. Sneaked in again on my belly. SAS training coming in handy. Mummy Cathy was awake. Her alarm had just gone off. Beep Beep Beep. So loud. The next thing, BOOM. I leapt like an athlete across the bed to land on mummy Cathy's head. OMG was she shocked. Mummy

Cathy never really gets cross with me though. She gave me a cuddle and then told me to get off the bed. Of course I didn't, I waited until she moved herself from the comfy bed. What can I do next? Mummy Cathy went for a pee and I waited patiently for the opportunity of the shoe room. Mummy Cathy next went into the water room. I don't like this room. There is a big long washing up bowl thing in there and it fills up with water. I was made to go in this once. Never again. It really did become a wet room after I had been in it. Horrible. Anyways, mummy Cathy went into the shoe room/clothes room. She couldn't decide what to wear today. I seized my chance. Got it, one of mummy Cathy's good sandals. Mummy Cathy was not happy. Mummy Cathy got dressed and ready for work and set about retrieving my new toy/sandal. It took a nice treat and a cuddle but I returned it to mummy Cathy in one piece. Any ways after munching my treat it is time to go back to bed as this is soooo early. Yawn. Well what a weekend I have had. It started with the fun with mummy Cathy. I then had a good lie in until daddy Kevin came home from work. We played and had cuddles and I checked out daddy Kevin's work bag top see if there were any left over's coming my way. Should have known better. Nothing. Daddy Kevin then went to pick mummy Cathy up and go to the market. They were not got long and they brought me back some kidneys from the butcher man. Mummy Cathy says the butcher man is kind and the meat is lovely and he gave me the kidneys and he doesn't even know me. Imagine what I could get he if knew me! After this, was meant to be an exciting afternoon. We were off in the car to visit daddy Kevin's cousin. Gillian lives in Australia but was back with her husband, Mark for a visit. Gillian's parents live in a small village in the Forest of Dean called White croft. Daddy Kevin got lost. We tried to use our mobiles to route check. NO signal. It was pouring down with rain and the afternoon didn't seem so much fun. I was meant to be allowed to run around with daddy Kevin but instead I hear mummy Cathy reluctantly saying I would have to stay in the car. Whoop Dee doo! Eventually we found the correct house. Daddy Kevin only spotted it because a huddle of people was sheltering in a huge double garage. We met Gillian and Mark. Gillian is absolutely beautiful. Tanned and really pretty. They have both now got slight Aussie accents but it was mixed with a Gloucestershire twang. It was like Gloucester meets home and away. It was lovely for mummy Cathy to meet them both as it was the first time she had met them and daddy Kevin hadn't seen them for 15 years so it was a good reunion. Nanny Brenda and grampy Dennis were still there. A lot of people had been and gone. Brenda and Dennis was aware mummy Cathy and daddy Kevin had to work until 1pm so couldn't have gotten there any earlier. Immediately questions of where have you been and why are you so late were being asked. Really, do you need to ask? We were sorry we had missed David and Colin but we had come to see Gillian and Mark. Sorry Colin and David this doesn't mean mummy Cathy and daddy Kevin didn't want to see you but they can always visit you another day. Hope this is okay. Happy birthday to Gillian and Norman for yesterday. Mummy Cathy and daddy Kevin took birthday cards for them both. Whoops light the touch paper and stand back. Nanny Brenda chirped up. I have given Gillian a card signed from us all. Mummy Cathy looked in dis belief. Why? Mummy Cathy said you do not need to do this. If we want to give cards we will do our own, if we do not give a card it is because we do not want too. Nanny Brenda then carried on to say that she says from Brenda and Dennis and family on all Christmas cards. Mummy Cathy was astounded. Mummy

Cathy said Daddy Kevin is 44 years old and she is 50 years old. Mummy Cathy says they are old enough to write their own cards at Christmas, which they do anyhow and daddy Kevin always delivers. Watching mummy Cathy's face from my front seat view in the car was brilliant. As if enough hadn't been said already. It wasn't over. Ohhhh noooo. Daddy Kevin was chatting with Gillian and the talk turned to her to dogs back home on Oz. They weigh around 35 kilo's each where as I way around 44 kilo's. Gillian was going to come to the car and pet me through the window. Nanny Brenda turned into health and safety. Don't put your hand in the car in case he bites you. Now I have NEVER EVER bitten anyone in my 6 years of life. I am NOT on any dangerous dog lists. I never even so much as growl or bark unless my water bowl needs filling or I need to go outside for a pee. I am a great big soft lump. Mummy Cathy was horrified. Why was my character being besmirched in such a way? When have I ever bitten Nanny Brenda? Why would she say such things about me? Later while mummy Cathy and daddy Kevin were visiting and chatting to a really nice lady about dog walking. Carol and Norman's dog Boe, who had been asleep, woke up on his own in his house. Boe doesn't like being on his own and started to cry and howl. Poor Boe. It is ok for me because I am a working dog and not on my own too much. Nanny Brenda again spoke. Troy is like that isn't he? Does Nanny Brenda know me at all!! I never howl and cry, bark or growl and I NEVER EVER EVER BITE!!!!! Mummy Cathy think nanny Brenda must have been in a bad mood or had one too many glasses of wine to be saying the things she was saying. Hope she didn't have a hangover. I think mummy Cathy has always known that nanny Brenda would rather that daddy Kevin had married a nice local girl. Well all of the local, girl's daddy Kevin met, couldn't see the wonderful man that he is and only saw the hearing aid. Daddy Kevin has told mummy Cathy that he was very unhappy at the time when they met. All of his friends were settled. Joanne had recently married. He was drinking alcohol more and more. Mummy Cathy and daddy Kevin are the perfect couple. They have saved each other's lives in more ways than one and they love me to pieces. After we got home, daddy Kevin gave me a bone that my Sis Michelle had gotten me. YUMMMY. What a weird stressful funny day it was. Sorry if I have upset anyone with this story but realllly, think before you speak peoples.

While daddy Kevin is at work, and not here to scowl at me. I will tell you a hilarious story from Saturday night/Sunday morning. Mummy Cathy and Daddy Kevin went out dancing. I think more drinking was done judging by daddy Kevin. Lol. They came home about 1 ish. People coming in at that time of night and waking me up. No consideration!!! I am sooo glad I woke up or I would have missed it. Mummy Cathy has some low alcohol lager bottles in the fridge and got herself one out. Daddy Kevin had a whisky. Mummy Cathy sat down at the kitchen table. Sensible. Daddy Kevin on the other hand stood up leaning on a work top. First of all he seemed okay but then it was clear he wasn't. He was still drinking his whisky mind. Mummy Cathy was a bit worried he was going to slide down the cupboards onto his bum. It wouldn't be the first time this has happened. Anyhow daddy Kevin finished his drink and poured himself another whisky. Now the fun starts. His eyes are shutting. He is grinning and pulling faces at mummy Cathy. Daddy Kevin then said a horse was sat behind him tapping his glass. What horse, I didn't see one come in. I hope it don't mess on the floor as I will get the blame!!! He then starts tapping himself on the face. Mummy Cathy asked, what are you doing?

Daddy Kevin replied, I am putting pins in my face. Say what!! Just to reassure people, there were no pins hurt in this story. Next he said did Nanny Brenda think I was Suarez with the biting. That has upset me. I am much better looking and a better footballer than he is. By now mummy Cathy is laughing sooo much and me I am splitting my sides. Mummy Cathy took me out for a pee pee before bedtime. She then set about trying to get daddy Kevin to go to bed. She didn't want to leave him downstairs as he would have fell asleep and ended up on the floor. Before now he has gone to sleep on my bed in my room. Bloody cheek! So mummy Cathy is telling daddy Kevin to get to bed. He wouldn't go before finishing his drink. Alky. Anyways eventually daddy Kevin said he would follow mummy Cathy up the stairs. Mummy Cathy had a pee etc and got into bed. It seemed like ages had passed and she saw that daddy Kevin still hadn't got into bed. She went looking for him. She opened the bedroom door and found daddy Kevin sat on the top stair, his head looking down the stairs but fast asleep. Mummy Cathy was sooo worried. She said you daft sod, you could have fallen head first down the stairs. She carefully helped him up and he went to bed. Daddy Kevin had something mummy Cathy called a hangover yesterday morning. You see the sort of thing I have to put up with. I got my own back though. Mummy Cathy let me into the bedroom yesterday morning and instead of jumping all over mummy Cathy, I jumped all over daddy Kevin. My turn to wake daddy Kevin up. Revenge is sweet...

Mummy Cathy has said she will meet herself coming backwards in a minute. What does she mean? How can she meet herself again in any direction? She does say some strange things. Another thing mummy Cathy has said is, she is as full as a tick. Ticks, aren't they the things Dr Bob picks of them celebrities (is that what they are) on that programme with Ant and Dec? She is strange. Mummy Cathy has given me another of my bones (thanks Sis) and I have been naughty apparently. I have taken it upstairs to munch on. It is nice upstairs with the thick carpet. Comfy to lie on. Mummy Cathy says it wouldn't be so bad but I don't stay in one place, I keeps moving. What mummy Cathy doesn't understand is there may be other predators watching me. We all know the mountain lion Fox) knows where I live. You can't be too careful!!! They say older ladies who choose younger men are mountain lions or cougars or some sort of big cats. Does this mean mummy Cathy is a tiger as well. Daddy Kevin is six years younger than mummy Cathy. Goooo mummy Cathy!!! My sister Michelle has put some of her old school photos on face book recently. Michelle looks just like Shannon. Lots of her old school friends have made comments to her. Mummy Cathy can remember when Michelle was about 8, she was in a country dancing show for parents and grand-parents to come and watch. Michelle looked lovely; mummy Cathy, like all of the parents was sooo proud of her little girl. Michelle's partner was a boy called Lucas. The show was done over 2 nights so that everyone could see it. All went well on the opening night. All children were perfect and danced really lovely, getting all of their steps right. On the 2nd night Michelle's partner Lucas was poorly and was a no show. Poor Michelle, do you know what they made her do. There was no under study or replacement for her. Michelle had to dance and pretend Lucas was there. She even had to hold her arms out in front and pretend they were holding hands. Mummy Cathy was sooo proud of her for this. Michelle was the best little girl in that show and the bravest. A true professional, the show must goooo on. Mummy Cathy and Michelle still laugh about this now and again. Daddy Kevin has forgiven me for telling you all about him being drunk on Saturday night. What I didn't say was, he had pretty much done about 50 hours work last week and was absolutely bloody exhausted. Sorry Daddy Kevin if I was mean to you. You were funny though!!

I have had a good evening sooo far with mummy Cathy. So far I have had 2 sausages, my last bone (thanks again sis) and cuddles from mummy Cathy. Could life get any better than this? Daddy Kevin are you going to match this? I dooo hope so....

Well what can I say? I have been quiet for a couple of days. Mummy Cathy wouldn't help me. How selfish is that!!! Mummy Cathy has had the afternoon on today and instead of doing something exciting like I would if I had an afternoon off. All she has done is cleaning. Washing, making bed, scrubbing toilet, polishing, hoovering and steaming floors. How boring is that. I would have at least chased my tail. I do not understand why I cannot catch it. I mean, I am really bendy. I can manage to lick my bottom but cannot catch my tail. Weird!! I had a lovely dream the other night. I was in a field and there were lots of rabbits. They weren't scared of me; in fact they were really friendly. We ran around the field chasing one another. It was just like in that film with Blackberry and Fiver. Mummy Cathy is singing Bright Eyes now. Mummy Cathy be quiet, I am trying to concentrate. Honestly, like I said, selfish. The bunnies took me to their houses underground. They had to dig extra big holes for me to squeeze through though. They didn't mind. I met all of the family. Grandparents, aunties and uncles, nephews and nieces. They have huge families. They were singing songs and dancing. They asked me if I was hungry, but I said I wasn't as they only had carrots. I reeeeallly do not like carrots. Granddad looked tasty though. Lol. I don't think they were related to Michelle's bunny. I did ask but they said they didn't know any town rabbits. They invited me to stay the night and sleep in their spare room. This was very nice of them I thought. Next thing I know, mummy Cathy is clattering about and woke me up. Again, selfish. I still haven't seen Eric. Do pigeons fly away for the summer and come back in the winter? I really am a bit worried about him. I know I didn't do anything to upset him as I am always kind and friendly. I hope a cat hasn't eaten him. Grrrrrr. Mummy Cathy has threatened that if it is a hot day tomorrow, I have got to have a shower in the garden. I cannot wait for this, NOT! It is not my fault I have filthy legs. It is my sister's fault. I have been eating bones this week and looked like I had been in the film Texas Chainsaw Massacre. They was yummy bones though. I was covered in blood. It has now dried on me. I have tried to clean it myself but not to mummy Cathy's satisfaction. What is mummy Cathy's problem? I do try to stay clean, it just never happens. At least if I get it out of the way tomorrow it will be done. Mummy Cathy says, until the next time!! I can't win, can I. I wonder if I will go to the park tomorrow and be let off my lead. I might find my rabbit friends. They were real. Just because I only saw them when I was asleep doesn't mean they don't exist. So long as I don't meet that mountain lion or David Attenborough I am safe. Daddy Kevin will be home soon. I wonder if he has eaten all of his sandwiches. Mmmm.

I am going to have a nap now before daddy Kevin gets home. I am tired after watching mummy Cathy rushing about....

Do you know what the worst part of my shower was. Mummy cathy made me pooh myself. Literally!!! How embarrassing is that....

I am in a bad mood today. To show this I have peed on daddy Kevin's sun lounger in the garden. Why am I in a bad mood? I don't really know, I just am. Yesterday, mummy Cathy had a migraine and so spent most of the day in bed. I can forgive her this as I know she was poorly. Daddy Kevin mean while was not poorly. He sat most of the day in front of the telly. He said he was sorting paperwork out. Rubbish he means for the burner in the garden. He didn't play with me or anything. Soooo boring. He was cross with me. On Saturday night I wanted to get on their bed for a sleepies as it was cooler in mummy Cathy's bedroom. I jumped on the bed and wouldn't let daddy Kevin in. Daddy Kevin dragged me off and ooooh dear. My spots on my chin had burst and left blood splattered all over the duvet. On daddy Kevin's side. He was soooo angry with mummy Cathy. She just smiled and said, poor Troycie. It is not his fault. It did look like an attack had happened. I cannot help my acne. I have tablets for it but they do not really help. Daddy Kevin washes my face regularly and mummy Cathy gives me my tablets so it is not my fault. Yesterday evening I was playing in the garden and a big bumbly bee was trying to steal pollen from mummy Cathy's runner beans. All of a sudden I was being shouted at to leave it. Whoops, too late. I jumped and it was in my mouth. Mummy Cathy was shouting at me to let it go. Oh no, I had captured it and it was mine. I didn't remember I am allergic to bumbly bees. Apparently when I was a puppy, I was stung by one and nearly died. My heart rate went down and was only saved by mummy Cathy. I dropped it and it didn't look too good so mummy Cathy had no choice but to squish it with her foot before I could grab it again. She went into the food room (kitchen) and fetched 2 of my anti histamine tablets and rammed them down my throat. Mummy Cathy tried to explain to me that bumble bees are good for the garden, they pollinate thee flowers and vegetables. They are not TOYS for me to play with. I think the bumbly bee must have stung me as I felt quite groggy all night after this and slept. I am soooo daft sometimes. Saturday was a lovely day for me. I had mummy Cathy and daddy Kevin all day to myself to play with. Apart from the shower in the garden and poohing myself 3 times. Soooo embarrassed. I cannot believe I told you all about this. Mummy Cathy and daddy Kevin must have felt sorry for me though because I did quite well for treats that day. Daddy Kevin is a lazy bones today. He has literally only just got up. Daddy Kevin is telling me off. I have peed on his deck chair, sat on his seat, to stop him sitting there obviously. I must snap out of my mood.......

Mummy Cathy has come home. She and daddy Kevin have taken Spiderman back home to Joey. Spiderman has been in hospital. He needed surgery to his leg. It was gruesome. He had been saving the world from baddies and his leg was hanging off. Magical surgery has happened and he is back in action. Go Spidey!!! There are a lot of slugs around because of the rain. I like playing with them but mummy Cathy doesn't. Apparently they can give me worms. I have to have horrible tablets for worms. They always make me sick. I only have to have them every 6 months so it is not too bad. Still horrible though. Daddy Kevin has gone to see Gym. He hasn't seen Gym in weeks. I think they must have fallen out over something. They must be friends again now though. Daddy Kevin has taken his big bag with him. Will it have treats in when he gets back do you think? Probably not. Daddy Kevin will have eaten it all, maybe shared with Gym. Daddy Kevin took me for a walk earlier in the rain. How mean was this. I am being treated quite badly at the moment. I am, not allowed to sleep on daddy Kevin's side of the bed. He hasn't taken me to meet Gym. We did share biscuits earlier though. Yummy there were. There is one bright side to this summer, and it is not the sunshine. Every year mummy Cathy and daddy Kevin go away, they fly off to another country. Usually Turkey. I like Turkey. We have this at Christmas and I get a leg to myself. Mummy Cathy takes the meat off the bone for me. OOOh I do love this. Is it Christmas in Turkey all of the time do you think? I have to go to what mummy Cathy calls Fat Camp. It's where dogs like me go to have a holiday and starve. The people at the all inclusive club I stay at are really nice. They cried last year when mummy Cathy and daddy Kevin fetched me. They have a big paddock for me to run around in. I say run around but I usually sprint in and then flop down for a rest. I am on holiday for a rest not for the sport. Mummy Cathy calls it fat camp because I always come home a bit slimmer. I lose my love handles and the fat socks from my ankles. Any way the bright side is, I get to stay home this year as they are not going anywhere and I do not need to go to fat camp. Sorreee everyone. I know I will be missed but maybe next year!! Mummy Cathy is starting to cook dinner now ready for when daddy Kevin comes home from seeing Gym. Mummy Cathy wishes she could have a friend like Gym where she could go to and have her dinner ready for when she comes home. Never mind mummy Cathy, at least you have me... I will not leave you on your own....

The sun is shining and I have just been out for my morning constitutional. (walkies) I am huffing and puffing. Daddy Kevin drags me along. We go for miles and miles. I cannot breathe. Daddy Kevin says it is because I am unfit. The cheek of it. It is because of my face shape says mummy Cathy. This must be true as mummy Cathy is never wrong. I was in such a bad mood yesterday. Daddy Kevin's fault. I cannot remember what he did or didn't do but I know it was daddy Kevin's fault.

Mummy Cathy had to go the dentist today. I do not know what a dentist is but mummy Cathy was sooo scared. Mummy Cathy had a filling come out on Sunday evening. It was 3 big lumps of grey stuff. It looked like stones from the garden. Mummy Cathy tells me not to eat them but clearly she must have to have bits in her mouth!!! Anyway mummy Cathy has had the filling replaced but may have to have the tooth taken out another day. Mummy Cathy also had to pay money for this. Pay money for pain. This doesn't seem right. Mummy Cathy and daddy Kevin do have nice gnashers, though not as nice as mine. I could do a doggy dental advert on the telly as my teeth sparkle in the sunshine. Mummy Cathy says it is because I gnaw on bones.

It has been a fabulous day today, mostly. Daddy Kevin has been home with me all day today. I was allowed a day off work to keep him company. He took me for a lonnnnng walk. I was shattered when we came back though. I needed a nap. Daddy Kevin went weeding in the back garden. He is redesigning our back garden where mummy Cathy grows her vegetables.

Daddy Kevin is really strange. He always likes to have a project on the go. His latest is the bottom of our garden, yet again. It has changed a few times over the years. Originally it was just steps down to a crazy paved area. Daddy Kevin built an arch way to walk through. Next all of the gravel (that I used to eat) was put down the bottom and a raised platform built. Daddy Kevin also built a gate to stop me eating the gravel. Grrr. Now all of the gravel is going, earth is being laid and the raised area flattened. This is where mummy Cathy will grow her vegetables. Not complicated at all!!

Daddy Kevin took a break from his weeding and design work to play ball with me. Mummy Cathy came in and they both played ball with me. They both had me running round and round. I am worn out now with a nice smiley face. True Happiness. Now I said this had been a fabulous day mostly. Daddy Kevin spoiled it. Daddy Kevin had hot dogs for his tea. This is not a scalding dog. No dogs were boiled in the cooking of daddy Kevin's tea. Apparently a hot dog is a sausage with onions in a bread roll. Strange name!! Now mummy Cathy cooked an extra sausage and put it on daddy Kevin's plate. Normally when this happens, daddy Kevin's lets it cool down and then gives it to moi. Well today. Do you know what he did? He ate it himself and then said that he didn't realize it had been meant for me. Mummy Cathy said, didn't you think it was odd when it wasn't in a roll. I really do not understand daddy Kevin sometimes. We had had such a lovely father and son day and then he does that. MEANY.

Daddy Kevin was going to see Gym again today but then couldn't be bothered. I don't think they have made friends properly yet. It might take a while. Daddy Kevin has gone swimming with his other friends tonight. He has gone to the pool with his stick again. No towel as usual but I suppose it is warm enough to just dry naturally tonight.

I am at home keeping mummy Cathy safe. I hope she doesn't watch anything scary or sad on the picture screen (television) on the wall. Sometimes when daddy Kevin does out she watches things that make her cry. Why does she watch these things? Mummy Cathy wakes me up sobbing and I have to go and give her a cuddle and make sure she is okay. Sometimes there are other dogs. It is strange though because I can see them, plain as day but when I go and search for them they are not there. Where do they vanish too? It is a real mystery!!!

Anyways, after my busy day and before mummy Cathy disturbs me I am off to dreamland.....

Mummy Cathy and daddy Kevin are both busily now helping me to prepare my book of stories to go to a publisher in America. I do not know where this is except that it too far for Daddy Kevin to walk me. It must be miles away because I do go on very long walks....

My pages so far have all been added to Microsoft word and are being spell checked and stuff ready to be emailed. This is sooo exciting for me. Everyone will be able to meet my family (are you excited sis?). There will be good things about them all and some not so nice things. Sometimes mummy Cathy gets really upset and cries about my brothers, Jon and Mike. Although on Friday last week in town, mummy Cathy said there was a coke stand and people were queuing up to have their names printed on to bottles of coca-cola. Mummy Cathy thought of my brother Jonathan. When he was 5, both my sister and Jonathan were taken to the seaside by their auntie and uncle. Whilst they were there, Michelle says she had the best donkey ride ever. Her uncle Butchie slapped her donkey on the backside and instead of a leisurely walk along the beach it bolted. Michelle absolutely loved it and still talks about it to this day. Any ways whilst they were there and in a gift shop. Michelle wanted a pen with her name on. Michelle. Of course this meant Jon wanted one also. Problem was there were none with Jon on. All of a sudden this little 5 year old chirped up and said Auntie Sylvie, this one is my name. It said Joan. This nick name has stuck with him all of this time. He hates being reminded. Ha-ha Joan boy.

I do not know where mummy Cathy gets the time to help me as well as look after the house and daddy Kevin. Mummy Cathy will always make time for others. Mummy Cathy also makes sure I have a clean water bowl and food. Daddy Kevin sometimes forgets. Tut tut daddy Kevin!!!

Some of the stories you read will be through my eyes. The things we see Troy do when he thinks we are not watching plus things regarding the family around Troy. I have been called a weirdo by some people for the telling of tales through Troy's eyes. I do not find it weird at all. Troy is a much loved member of our family and is treated and spoilt as such. People through the ages have always treated dogs as family members. I just take it to the extreme. If you do not like this then the answer is a simple one. Put the book down and do not read it!!!

Troy is a fabulous boy. He is a big boy who at first glance, if you didn't know him can appear quite scary. Appearances can be deceptive as Troy is as the saying goes as daft as a brush. Troy is cuddly and affectionate and hasn't a bad bone in him. He really only barks when he wants his water bowl cleaned out or wants his dinner. Troy doesn't like to drink out of water bowl if it appears to be dirty. When I say dirty, I mean he has just drank from it and it has dog drool in it. Troy does drool a lot and I do mean a lot. At meal times. He sits next to us. He doesn't do anything except move from me to Kevin and doggy drool hangs from his mouth. Every now and then you can hear Kevin thanking Troy for wiping his mouth on his leg or arm. Troy is really sneaky about it though, you usually do not see it coming. The only time you will hear troy growl, isn't really a growl. It is when he is playing games with Kevin. Man games. They play rougher than I can play as they play the rough and tumble games. Father and son stuff. Like fathers playing wrestling with their boys. Troy's little stumpy tail whirls round like a helicopter rotor. You can see the happiness in his face. These games do not last long and there is never really a winner as Troy normally gives up with exhaustion. Troy does enjoy his nap time!!!

One of the funniest things with Troy and meal times is. Kevin is usually in the lounge when I am cooking a meal. When the food is on plates and on the table, I just shout dinner is on the table. The first person in the kitchen and sat to the table is Troy. Troy understands soooo much of what is said around him. He is like a child in many respects. We sometimes have to use coded words so that Troy will not be interested in what we are doing. Troy also understands that some foods are wrapped in foil for freshness. This means that whenever Troy sees foil it equals food and he also assumes it is for him. This is Kevin's teachings mainly as he takes sandwiches etc to work wrapped in foil. On occasions, some get brought home and guess who is waiting to share any left over's, Troy.

We do have to watch his weight as he is prone to carry the odd pound or two more than he should. This means diets and frequently he is having to diet. Troy has regular health checks though and is in very good health. Except for his acne, his hay fever, his alopecia and his allergy to bee stings. The list goes on with Troy but as I said he does have regular health check and takes his medication regularly. He takes anti-biotics, steroids and hay fever tablets. As I said Troy is like a child. Troy is our child, our baby. We would not change him for the world!!

Both Kevin and I work full time which would normally mean Troy is left on his own a lot of the time. We are all very lucky as we both work shifts which means that a lot of the time someone is at home and Troy gets the company which is how it should be. Troy craves company and although he doesn't howl or bark when he is on his own the excitement and love we receive when we return is unbelievable. Troy always brings one of his favourite toys to greet us with. Troy normally greets meet with what I have named his babies. These are his soft toys. Troy has a black, yellow and pink baby. These are the babies he sleeps with. Troy has a toy box which is absolutely laden with toys. Some are really old and Kevin says some of them should be thrown away. Every time we think okay, the old chicken which is torn and tatty can be thrown away; Troy retrieves it from his toy box for another tugging game. Troy also has his own bedroom. Yes his own bedroom. It has a leather two seater sofa, complete with duvet for sleeping. He has his food and water dishes and his toy box in it. This is where Troy goes if he just wants quiet time. Especially if I am hovering. He isn't a fan of the vacuum cleaner. When my two sons Jonathan and Michael both lived at home, Troys room had a gate across the door way. Troy was rarely ever in his room with the gate closed. It was mainly for his own safety. The boys used to regularly go out and drink too much. We were always worried they would come home and leave the front door open and that Troy would wander off. Troy is not a street wise dog and is rarely allowed off his lead. Now that the boys have flown the nest the gate has been removed and is only replaced if we are decorating or have visitors who do not appreciate being covered in dog hair and drool. Being covered in dog hair and drool is now part of living with Troy. We rarely wear our good clothes around the house and do sometimes appear to look like tramps. As I have previously stated we wouldn't have Troy any other way.

I was sat watching Troy sleep last night in the lounge. Legs all spread out. He was dreaming. All four of his legs were moving as if walking or running, his mouth and nose were twitching so I guess food was involved somewhere. He is so funny. People say dogs relive the best bits of their days through dreams. If this is so, I wish we could tap into troy's dreams and review his best bits. Too us, being with Troy and each other are the best bits. We are a close knit little unit. We do not really get many visitors and so our lives revolve around each other. Prior to adopting Troy our house was spotless. I cannot stand, even now to have magazines and newspapers scattered around. My daughter Michelle is exactly the same. I do not like ornaments as I just call them dust collectors. I have always thought that when I pass away who the hell is going to want them. Answer would be nobody. I do have a china hedgehog pushing a wheelbarrow. My son Jonathan bought it for me years ago and that does live and always will in my cabinet. This is purely sentimental. No more though please!! Now having said this I do like crystal and have a small collection of bits. They also live in the cabinets along with crystal decanters that I have picked up at car boot sales. Car boot sales are a hobby of mine. Kevin drops myself and my daughter Michelle off on the weekends and picks us up when we have finished. We are normally laden up like pack horses. Kevin just rolls his eyes and says what the hell have you bought this week?

Anyhow, back to the spotless house before the adoption of troy the destroyer. Now, I do not think there is a room you can enter without a bit of Troy being in there with you. No matter how many times the floors are hovered and steamed you will always find a dog hair. We have two lemon leather sofas in the lounge. One has a duvet on and has become Troy's personal sofa. This is his real bedtime sofa. Sometimes he curls up into a ball using only one half of the sofa and other times he literally consumes the sofa and hangs off the end. I f he is feeling mischievous, which is an awful lot of the time. Troy will wait until you are about to sit down on the three seater and then lunge at the seat and take over the space. He then sits tall and proud knowing that he has won and will not be removed. It is always Kevin or me that sit elsewhere. Who said an Englishman's home is his castle. Wrong. An Englishman's home belongs to the dog!!

At the moment I am writing this in deathly silence. Kevin has taken Troy to his parent's house for a visit. It is so strange. No Troy bounding around searching for food or disturbing wanting to play ball in the garden. The house seems to quiet. It is not nice here without Troy. I know it is only a couple of hours but it brings thoughts of what life would be like without him and believe me these are not pleasant thoughts. I shall push these thoughts away or I will be sobbing.

Back to Troy as he is now and how he was as a pup.

As a youngster Troy the destroyer was turning out to be a very apt name for Troy. You couldn't turn your back on him for one second without him getting into mischief. If a tea towel was left on a work top in sight of Troy, it would then be in his mouth and down the garden being what we now call killed. If you were lucky enough to get it back in one piece it would be full of rips and holes. Dead for sure. I have lost count of the amount of oven gloves lost in battle. Sometimes when you are in the kitchen you just totally forget about Troy and his murderous ways and leave things lying around. I once owned a beautiful bright pink mobile phone. I stupidly left it on the kitchen table, walked to our local paper shop. As I was walking back I remembered my beautiful pink phone and where I had left it. As I walked through the front door, there was Troy. As happy as happy can be. Phone smashed beyond recognition. All that was left was the sim card. It was too late to reprimand him as he wouldn't have understood why he was being told off. I just had to clear the bits up and prepare to tell Kevin. Kevin just raised his eyebrows at Troy and bought me another phone with the warning of do not leave it lying around.

Television controls have been chewed and unusable and so replaced. Countless newspapers and magazines, socks and well all sorts really have been murdered. You have to remember that when we adopted Troy, although he was still only four months old, he was already bigger than most fully grown boxer dogs and was still growing. Through all of this he was still our baby.

By far the worst and most worrying object to be eaten was a rubber glove. One of the latex types used when colouring hair. Yes it was mine. It was not left on a work top but high on a window sill above the kitchen sink. Somehow, even today we are unsure of how Troy managed to grab it. We chased him into the garden, offering all manner of treats whilst still trying to be in control. The next thing was a gulp. Troy had swallowed the glove. We had to ring our emergency vet and take him immediately to have the glove removed. What goes in must come out we were told. Otherwise it could cause all manner of damage to him intestines. They gave Troy an injection and we had to wait while it took effect. After half an hour of walking him around the vet car park, the vet was discussing surgery to remove the glove as it definitely needed to be removed and asap. All of a sudden as if Troy had heard about the up and coming surgery he started wretching. Out came the glove, still in one piece. Did I want it back? Ummm no, I passed on that one.

Troy is no stranger to surgery and vet's waiting rooms. His first operation was shortly before his first birthday and he was due to be neutered. Now all you men who may be reading this will have sympathy with Troy. It should have been simple surgery. As Paul (the best ever vet and Troy's favourite) had said a quick in and out job. It turned out to be far from simple. One of Troy's testicles hadn't dropped and so a search had to be done to find and retrieve it. It had got stuck right up and tucked away. It apparently wasn't an easy or straight forward operation but thankful to Paul it was all sorted. If a testicle doesn't drop and is left inside a dog it can lead to cancer in later life.

Troy's next surgery was his eyes. Troy has what was called diamond eye shape and if left untreated could lead to blindness. Troy was referred to a doggy eye specialist in Birmingham. This is about an hour's drive away from where we live for plastic surgery. He needed the eye shape altered so that his tear ducts could perform correctly. This was a fifteen hundred pound operation which had to be paid for. A massive thank you to Tesco pet insurance who have always covered

Troy's operations and ailments without question. What a sad day this was for us, walking around a strange area whilst waiting for our baby to be well enough to come home. When we received the call that the surgery had gone well and that we could pick him up. He looked so sorry for himself. He was wearing one of those lamp shade hood things to stop him from scratching at his stitches. When we got Troy home, we had been told as with his previous operation that Troy would still be sleepy from the operation. As on the last occasion with anatheasic Troy was not in the least sleepy but back to his usual, well almost usual self. This time though he was wearing an enormous lamp shade on his head. Troy suffers with clumsiness at the best of times. He kind of barges past things that he should maybe walk around. Troy was hitting everything, but mainly it was him and us who were suffering. Troy couldn't understand why he was unable to get close to us for a cuddle and was really not a happy chappie. We made the decision to remove the lampshade. Our legs were bearing the marks of being slashed. We decided that as soon as we saw him scratching at his stitches we would replace the lampshade. Troy is not and was not stupid. Not once did he even attempt to scratch at his eyes. His eyes healed and we took him to see Paul who gave him a big cuddle and thumbs up on his handsome new looking eyes. Troy is a handsome chap.

His next operation shouldn't have been necessary. As I have explained, Kevin does shift work although now for a different company. At this time he would start work at twelve midday and finish at twelve midnight. On a Friday and Saturday night I would wait up for him. Troy would run around with his tail wagging as he heard the key turn in the lock. On this one particular night, Troy was let out in the garden for a pee.

Troy is always hunting for things in the garden at night so we have to be careful with him. Slugs, snails, toads have all been brought in as gifts in the past. Anyway this night he seemed to have a sniff around and came in and led down for the night. All of a sudden I could see blood spots on the floor, more and more was appearing. I panicked and ran to Troy to see where the blood was coming from. It was his mouth and it was pumping out. Troy had cut his tongue on a leaf. How could a leaf do this much damage? It was a small cut but quite deep. Again a call was made to the emergency vet. It was now one thirty in the morning and we were bungling Troy wrapped in a towel and taking him to the vet. He was quickly examined and given an injection to stop the bleeding and to help his blood clot normally. It was a waiting game now. The bleeding wasn't stopping. He was given another injection and we were told we would have to leave Troy over night to be checked and that if the bleeding didn't stop he would have to put to sleep again and have stitches. Poor Troy, another operation. The morning came and we were called to pick Troy up. He had needed stitches. Troy was so pleased to see us and to come home. Again we were told he may need to wear a lampshade if he started to scratch at the stitches. Troy again isn't stupid. He didn't wear the lampshade again. We now have no plants or leaves in the garden for Troy to do damage to himself with. This wasn't a conscious decision by us. It was all Troy's own handiwork.

I have had such fun at nanny Brenda's today. I have peed on her flowers as I always do. Nanny Brenda laughs at me through gritted teeth. Nanny Brenda is not my biggest fan when I pee on her flowers. I was going to say Clematis but it sounded rude so we will leave it as flowers. I have run up and down their massive garden until I just flopped down on the grass. Nothing and no-one can move me when I flop down like this, unless there is food around. They have endless cups of tea. I do not see the point of tea. Boiled water not cold as I have it. Then the water is poured on to these funny leaves in bags and changes colour to a brown almost muddy liquid and then they drink it. Yuck. Nanny Brenda then sometimes saves these bags and makes things with them and people think I am weird!!! Nanny Brenda is always painting material and sewing stuff. She makes pillow cases and pictures and well she starts so many things a lot of it never gets finished or sees the light of day. I can see where mummy Cathy gets the term half a job from. Mummy Cathy sometimes calls daddy Kevin half a job. Daddy Kevin starts a few different tasks and mummy Cathy sometimes has to nag at him (which makes him cross) to finish them. Grampy Dennis is the same. Mummy Cathy noticed a long time ago that the wall paper in the kitchen had small spots on it that the paint brush had missed. Sorreeee and also an edging piece hadn't been glued to edge of a work surface. Again, half a job. Sorreeee mummy Cathy for repeating what you say, but you realllly shouldn't have said it with my flappy ears listening!!

Nanny Brenda and grampy Dennis are as fit as fleas though. Fleas must be fit because they do an awful lot of jumping. They could be in the Olympic high jump team or the long jump team. They would be a sure bet for a medal. Just to let you all know. I do not have fleas. Mummy Cathy puts this liquid stuff she buys from the vet on my neck so that I do not get these little trespassers. Anyways back to nanny Brenda and grampy Dennis. They do lots of things to keep fit. Remember they are really old compared to me. They are both in their seventies. They go line dancing, country and western, swimming and don't forget they go white ball hunting (golf). Mummy Cathy says fair play to them for doing all of this, it helps keep them young. Young I have already given their ages away, Whoops.

Daddy Kevin has eaten some bread rolls while we were there. I gave my best starving puppy look and yes he shared. I have also eaten the snacks mummy Cathy packed for me. Thank you mummy Cathy.

Daddy Kevin has brought a birdie table home with us today. Mummy Cathy had noticed in on the floor at the bottom of the garden (where the Poddington peas live) and asked daddy Kevin to see if Nanny Brenda and grampy Dennis would let her have it as it wasn't being used. Eric will be so pleased. He will be able to bring the family round and have a proper sit down meal. It will be like a restaurant for him. Oooh I am so excited. I can't wait to show Eric and to meet his family. I wonder if he will show me his holiday photos. I hope not, although I am interested in where he has been. It is really boring looking at other peoples holiday pics. Sorreee to all the people who like to show off holiday photos. You carry on if it makes you happy.

I was saying about my afternoon at Nanny Brenda's. I have now worked out why they have not got blinds or full length net curtains at their window. First of all I have to explain that they have just got a half net which only covers half the window, leaving the top half of the window clear. While I was there and sat in my window seat watching the world go by. Nothing much to see from my point of view until a big lorry turned up with a sort of crane thing attached. Well here is where the clear window comes into its own. Both Nanny Brenda and grampy Dennis were at the window like rats up a drain pipe. Do rats really run up drain pipes? I have never seen any. Mummy Cathy is glad about this. Faces almost pressed to the glass. Nanny Brenda was almost shoving me from my seat for a better view. A neighbour over the road has been having some work done and the rubble etc was being taken away in the big collection bags. It must have been a sight to behold Nanny Brenda, grampy Dennis and me all nosying out of the window as if we had never seen a lorry before. I expect grampy Dennis will go over and inspect whatever work has been done and report back to nanny Brenda.

We brought the birdie house home with us. Well done to mummy Cathy for spotting it. Mummy Cathy said she saw it in pieces on the ground a while ago and put it together and stood it up so she knew it was ok. Funny thing is though the next time she saw it. It had been taken apart again. Grampy Dennis said he was going to throw it away as it has a small crack on the birdie house roof. I am sure Eric will not mind. Daddy Kevin has set it up at the bottom of the garden to encourage Eric to visit me more often. I do hope he does. It will help him put the weight back on that he has lost while on his holiday. Mummy Cathy has been down to the birdie house today and put some bread on it for him and his family. I do not mind if other little birds come and visit, except for those pesky seagulls. They are too big and mean. They have nasty little eyes which don't seem very friendly. Mummy Cathy sometimes throws bread over the fence at the little school by us in the evenings and the little birds and Eric and his family do not stand a chance. Those pesky seagulls always get there first and gobble down the bread. They are just sooo greedy. I think I will call it Troy's Bistro.

Mummy Cathy and daddy Kevin went to somewhere called Mine head yesterday. I think they must have gone separately though because mummy Cathy came back dark brown and well daddy Kevin didn't. I mean he did come back but not dark brown. Mummy Cathy sat on the beach sunbathing and daddy Kevin went to watch the footie. Eric has been back a few times and looks back to his usual weight. I think he must have been breathing in last week or wearing good under wear. Whilst in Mine head, Daddy Kevin saw lots of people he knew. Weird as that normally happens in Weston super mare. Mummy Cathy is feeling really proud of herself. Mummy Cathy is the first person to admit she doesn't like or do sports. Well along time ago when Cheltenham had a ten pin bowling alley. Mummy Cathy beat my brothers, Jonathan and Michael and daddy Kevin on a basket ball shooting machine. Michael spent the rest of the evening there trying to beat her score. He didn't manage though. Ha-ha, Michael. Well yesterday, breaking news. Mummy Cathy beat daddy Kevin on a basket ball shooting game three times. Daddy Kevin made her play three times as he was so miffed. He is soooo competitive; Mummy Cathy wasn't even trying which made it worse for daddy Kevin. In the third and final game mummy Cathy had 52 points and daddy Kevin had 28 points. Sorry daddy Kevin but I am laughing. Beaten by a girly who is rubbish at sport!!!! I hope your friends don't read this. Lol. Mummy Cathy is taking my sis and the beautiful Shannon, Eleanor and the man Joey to Evesham on Wednesday so it had better be sunny for them. Daddy Kevin has gone out tonight to watch men in the pool with sticks tonight. It must be like a swim gala or something. I have been thinking about this and the water cannot be very good for the sticks and I thought it would rot them. Maybe one day he will take me and then I will be able to see exactly what goes on there!!

Another British cloudy day. I hope the sun makes an appearance tomorrow as mummy Cathy is going on a day trip with Michelle, Shannon, Joey and Eleanor. I am not allowed to go. Apparently they are not going in the car but on a coach. What mummy Cathy calls a proper day out. I have been allowed a couple of days off work this week as daddy Kevin is home. I cannot work with daddy Kevin wandering around getting in my way. He lounges around like he owns the place. Lol. Mummy Cathy is still reminding him that she is basketball queen and that daddy Kevin is the Llllllooooossser. Mummy Cathy said 3-0. Not seen Eric today but to be honest I haven't really looked for him. I have had a lazy day just lying around. Daddy Kevin took me for a walk earlier. That tired me out. It really is more tiring when you do nothing at all. Daddy Kevin is off out again tonight. He has quite a good social life. (Whatever that is). I am just repeating what I have heard mummy Cathy say. He doesn't come home sooo chatty on a Tuesday night though because he drives and so doesn't drink alcohol. Daddy Kevin is meeting his friends to play to pool competition matches. I am sooo confused. Firstly they play in a pool with 2 matches. Surely the matches will not light in a pool. Secondly isn't it dangerous to play with matches. I hope they have a responsible adult watching over them!!!! Now any little white balls reading this. I am giving you a warning. Daddy Kevin and grampy Dennis are going white ball hunting tomorrow. I am giving you all the chance to find suitable hiding places. Try the long grass, the sand pits and the watery bits, ponds are all good hiding places. Choose you hiding places well and do not be frightened. Daddy Kevin is a kind man. He will let you escape. I am off to the land of nod now. Little white balls, I will try and help you further if I can. Remember it is a cruel world out there. Stay Safe!!!.....

I have just been told off by mummy Cathy. I asked her if we could try lighting matches in water the same as daddy Kevin is doing. Mummy Cathy has told me in no uncertain terms that we cannot as it is extremely dangerous and that MATCHES are not to be played with. I hope you are reading this Daddy Kevin!!!!

This is a story from mummy Cathy. What a wonderful day was had yesterday. I was so tired from it; I was in bed by 8pm until 10 am today. How lazy is this!!!

I took my daughter and 3 of my grand-children on an outing. We caught the marchants coach to town and then the Astons coach to Evesham. We spent a wonderful day at Evesham's Abbey Park. There is so much for children of all ages, and I do mean all ages to do there. The sun shone at times and we were lucky to escape all rain until we arrived back in Cheltenham at 5pm. It was a joy to see Shannon, Joseph and Eleanor laughing and smiling so much. Some brilliant photos were taken of all 4 children on the swings and the trampoline. Sandwiches, crisps and biscuits were devoured at speed. Sorry to the ducks, nothing was left for you. A woman attempted to get the better of us by issuing her orders as to whose turn it was on the twisty swing. Message to her. Do not mess with us as you will not and did not win. You cannot expect to argue with an 11 year old and not expect mum and Nan to not get involved. Pick on someone who will argue back!!! The Abbey Park is truly an amazing place to spend an afternoon. There is a huge sandpit with a fort in the centre, a trampoline, a big tubular slide, water fountains which children operate by stamping on with their feet, a massive sort of wooden spider web climbing frame and much more. The children sat eating ice-creams whilst mum and Nan had a cup of tea. I am still smiling now at the laughs coming from Michelle and children on the big bowl swing as they were all in it together and Michelle with her girls on the trampoline. No one batted an eye lid as mum and children played together. We set sadly off for the coach home and realized we were further away than we thought. Olympic sprinter Shannon set off at sped and stood in coach door way as the rest of us sauntered back to the coach. Well done Shannon!!! On we got and sat in the same seats and luckily found Eleanor's cardigan which was forgotten when we got off. A lady coach driver on return trip decided to do a detour down a narrow road. Whoops no room to turn round and stuck. Took her 10 minutes and a few choice words to back the coach back on to main road. I bet she won't do that again. All in all it was a brilliant old fashioned day out and a good time had by all.....

Well I was soooo tired when I woke up this morning. Mummy Cathy says it is because I never lie still for more than 10 minutes when I am asleep. Daddy Kevin says I am just like mummy Cathy, a bloody wriggler. Michelle, do you remember the wrigglers on telly when you were little. They were ugly/cute little people on kids TV.

Daddy Kevin went to his pool AGAIN last night. Daddy Kevin is trying to explain to me that it is a game played on a table with lots of little balls. Some are red and some are yellow and one white ball. You have to hit the balls into holes with your stick and the whit ball. Sounds similar to golf to me. Chasing balls down holes, except for the table bit. Anyways, daddy Kevin one lots of games last night and his team have one something called the league. Does this mean daddy Kevin's team is like Man Utd? Daddy Kevin has won about 5 trophies this year. Mummy Cathy has said they will all have to go up stairs with the others. Mummy Cathy is a Meany sometimes. Daddy Kevin is so proud of all of his trophies and mummy Cathy makes him put them out of sight in what is called the grandkids room. Mummy Cathy is proud of daddy Kevin; it is just that she cannot stand clutter that sits collecting dust!!

Daddy Kevin played golf the other day. Even after the warning I gave to all of the little balls, they still didn't manage to get away. In fact daddy Kevin managed to find some other little balls that had managed to escape on a different day. They must have been so frightened. Daddy Kevin is a kind man and so he will not hurt the little hostages. He will take them out another day and let them escape. I will try to let them know which day this will be.

I am going out for a walk now. Daddy Kevin has said it is going to rain so we need to get going.....

Back to Mummy Cathy now.

I will give you an insight of my life now. I am 50 years old. Almost 51 years now.

I met my first husband when I was just 15 years young. I had gone to a working men's club with my sister. She was meeting her boyfriend there and dragged me with her. I hated it. I was being pestered by a bloke who was years older than me and thought by buying me a dubonnet and lemonade it gave him the green light for other things. It just wasn't happening. When I told him where to go he was not happy. Not happy at all. This blonde haired lad and his family took pity on me and gave me a lift. God knows where my sister had gone. Anyway I started seeing this lad and we became an item.

I should have seen the signs from the start but when you are young you don't realise what the signals mean. Bullyish and possessive I wasn't allowed to see my friends. I wasn't allowed to wear make-up or clothes he didn't approve of. I thought this is what it was like when being in a relationship. My school work immediately slipped. I went from an A grade student to truanting and leaving school with no qualifications to my name. My mum had no control over me at all. She must have been devastated with what I was doing with my life. She made no secret that she disliked him. Me though I was in love. I was smitten.

After school I went to work in a factory called Lynotype-Paul. We used to solder circuit boards there and I loved it. I made some really good friends there, some I still have to this day. I wasn't allowed to mix with them alone outside of work though. He thought if I wasn't with him then I must be going out on the pull. I had absolutely no self esteem what so ever. I belonged to him. I would have and did do everything I was told to do by him.

When I was 17 years old, still really only a child myself I found I was pregnant. I was bringing shame into my family. A single mother. Of course I was keeping my baby. In my pretend world we would get a flat and live happily ever after. So long as I did as I was told.

Years went by in the blink of an eye. Day after day, year after year. I had three beautiful children, whom I wouldn't swop for the world. They were my world. They are what got me through life. I did leave him once. I went to stay with my sister and her husband but he persuaded me to come home with the words, I will change. Nothing changed. He went out drinking a lot of the time. He would have 9 pints on a Sunday lunch session at the pub, come home and eat his dinner and then go to sleep. This meant the kids would have to be quiet or all hell would break out. He also had hobbies. None of them were cheap hobbies either. Fishing, top of the range equipment. Golf. Top of the range clubs. Shooting. Top of the range shotgun. Where did the money come from. I was given house keeping money, in which to pay the rent, pay bills and get food. We were always behind with the rent. I never ever ate lunch so that I could keep the food in the house for my kids. I always tried to make sure they never went without. I would get their clothes on the never never. (weekly). My mum always helped out with the kids especially her little angel Michelle. I do not know how I would have coped without my mum. Wierdly thoughI never confided in anyone about how bad my life was. I did try to end my life once though. I took some tablets and realised it wasn't what I wanted to do and rang an ambulance.

Through out my married life I suffered mental and physical abuse. I was an expert in pretending to be happy. He was always careful where my bruises would be. Always where they wouldn't be seen. I put up with affair after affair until one day in 1999 I had finally had enough and kicked him out. I was so frightened. What was going to happen to me and the boys now would be a whole new way of life hopefully a happier one.

I ended up living in a rough are. The council man warned me about needles being left lying around the area as he gave me my keys. It didn't matter we would be safe behind our own front door.

Things were on the up. I met my lovely Kevin in the year 2000. Kevin treated me with respect and kindness and love. I found it really hard being part of a proper couple at first as I had never been treated like this. Kevin would ask where or what I wanted to do and I would just say, I don't mind you choose. I didn't have to look at the floor all of the time now. I could actually look around and smile at people without accusations or a punch coming my way.

Kevin suffered in a different way for daring to be with me. Sixteen car tyres were slashed on Kevin's car. White gloss paint thrown over the windscreen of the car. We even caught him doing it one evening and the police were useless. They did nothing. He had been cautioned a couple of years prior to this for beating to pulp a taxi driver. We were in Henley in Arden with friends. He got drunk and attacked the driver of our taxi. Reason being that the taxi driver had asked him to stop swearing. No-one ever told him what to do. Everyone was scared of him and so no one would admit what he had done. The police didn't speak to me, I wish that they had. I knew then that Kevin truly loved me and my children because it would have been so easy for him to walk away. He didn't he stayed. Thank you Kevin.

There is a lot more I could tell you about my life before and after Kevin but it would take so long and to be honest it is not a pretty story. So I will leave it there. Maybe one day if I am asked I will tell the whole story.

While I have said I will not tell the uglier side to my life I do feel I would be glossing over things without this chapter of events.

I was estranged from my daughter and her family for 10 long years. You may think this is odd as we are so very happy together now. There are things left unsaid between us, things Michelle struggles to talk about. Things that she feels unable to talk about with anyone. There are two people who whom are aware of this. One being her brother Jonathan, and the other being her father. I did question her once, after Jonathan blurted the truth out and she gave me a look and no more was said. Earlier this year, Michelle and myself had an evening out together and I again asked her the question. Were you abused by your father and her face crumpled and the truth came out. She is petrified of her father. I am mortified by these facts as of course I blame myself. Any mother in this situation would blame themselves. Why didn't she tell me, how could I have not known. It all made sense with how she would stay at friends houses or her grandparents at every given opportunity. Michelle will not report him as she is getting on with her life and is ashamed of this part of her life. Me, I am just having to live with it. I cannot report my ex husband without Michelle's backing.

Last year I had my 50th birthday and a party was arranged. All family were there to witness my embarrassment. I invited all of my work colleagues and relatives from Kevin's side. Thankfully he has a large family as apart from one work friend and a couple of other friends no one else turned up. I should have been saddened by this but I wasn't. What saddened me was that my eldest son and his partner were a no show. His excuse was that he had no money and would have had to walk to the venue. Approximately a 20 minute walk. I did have a brilliant evening even though a black shadow was descending upon me.

I spoke with my son regarding the party and all I received back were lame excuses, such as, did I expect him to walk, did I expect him to come with no money. In the past whenever he has needed money he has never given it a second thought that the bank of Kevin wouldn't give to him. We have bailed Jonathan out of so much debt in the past and never asked or have got a thank you. On the night of my party Kevin taxi'd Michelle and her crew to the venue and would have willingly given a lift to Jonathan. We would also have paid for drinks if this had been an issue for him. All that we received were threats and abuse. When Jonathan broke up with Kayleigh, the mother of his first born. We were there to help him through this. Now he does not know or seem to care where this little girl is or how she is getting on. Like a lot of people his reaction seems to be. Out with the old and in with the new. Jonathan moved into a flat with his partner Sarah and their little boy. Kevin, myself and Sarah's dad were their helping with the decorating and things. As most people in their 1st homes do not have everything they need. Sarah's family and us rallied round and got them the things they needed. Microwave, fridge etc. We received a call from Jonathan telling us he no longer wanted anything from us and could we come and collect the fridge. My husband is a 44 year old man. Okay he is fit and takes care of himself. Jonathan was 29 now 30 years of age. Jonathan stood in his doorway speaking very quietly and threatening. He put his face up to Kevin's in a threatening manor. Kevin has never hit or been in a fight in his life and is the most gentle person I know. How could Jonathan behave in this way. Kevin had only ever done his best for Jonathan. Jonathan up to this point from the age of fifteen had had no contact from his dad. This was his dad's choice. Again out with the old and in with the new. Regarding the threats, I was left in tears and we left. My family was falling apart. At this time my younger son was also starting to be abusive and blaming me for everything he didn't like in his life. Michael has had contact throughout his life with his dad. I say contact, this is to be taken with a large pinch of salt. None of my three children have ever received a birthday or Christmas card from their father. He did invite Michael to have a drink with him on his 21st birthday. This resulted with Michael being admitted to hospital with alcohol poisoning. Where was his dad at the hospital to see the results of his actions, nowhere to be seen. Michael is now living in his own flat. I see him regularly with food parcels and he still comes to me when he has a problem and for his Sunday lunch. Michael says that no one does Sunday lunch like his mum.

On December 21st last year I was in a really bad place. The black cloud had descended and I couldn't see a way forward without all of my children. I took about 150 strong painkillers with a bottle of wine and ended my life. Kevin had been unaware of my true state of mind. I hadn't been to work for two months as my doctor was signing me off with depression. I even told my doctor that suicide was on my mind. I was leaving the house at normal times, wandering the streets until I knew the house would be free and then I would go home. Life was not good. On the evening of the 21st I knew I was ready to go. I knew Kevin would not be home until three in the morning as he would be working overtime. I took the tablets and drank the wine and descended into unconsciousness. The next thing I knew was that Kevin was home and ringing an ambulance. He dragged me from the sofa and was forcing me to vomit. Kevin had come home from work early and saved my life again. I was truly lucky. I do not remember much of this as I floated in and out of sleep. I do no though that if Kevin hadn't come home I wouldn't be here today.

Today my life is back in perspective. I do not at this time have contact with Jonathan. One day I know this will change. Jonathan takes no responsibility for anything and only seems to believe what he wants to believe. I hope one day he will back his sister and that the truth can come out so that she can truly live her life. As for Michael, he is doing well in his flat and is lovely to see him happy. He needed to be in his own place to sort himself out. He wasn't thrown out as many people seem to think. It was a decision we all discussed and helped him with. Again as with Jonathan we were there providing him with everything he needed. This is just what parents do. I love all of my children equally and without question. Someone once said to me. When a child is born they make your arms ache and as they grow up they make your heart ache...

Anyway back to happier times.

Kevin and I bought the house where we still live in 2001 and were married in 2002. We are lucky enough to go on holiday abroad every year. Previously before Kevin I had never owned a passport let alone been on a plane. We went on a cruise for our honeymoon. I have been extremely blessed with meeting Kevin and finding true love and happiness.

Our family life is compete with Troy the destroyer and my wonderful grandchildren.

I will now hand you back to Troy and his stories.

It is nearly Daddy Kevin's birthday. I have sneaked out a couple of times to wandr round the shops. I do not know what to buy Daddy Kevin. I have to be careful because if Mummy Cathy sees me out she goes absolutely mad at me. Remember I am only 6 years old. Nearly 7. Mummy Cathy says I am not old enough yet to go shopping on my own!!! Mummy Cathy has bought Daddy Kevin a tablet. Why would you buy a tablet, is he poorly or something. I would know if he was poorly wouldn't I. It is a big tablet, I do not know how he will swallow it? Daddy Kevin sits with it on his lap touching a screen. Maybe he is trying to make it smaller?

It is also Eleanor's birthday this weekend. She is going to be 7 years old. Mummy Cathy and Daddy Kevin are going to something called a disco. I am not allowed to go. Mummy Cathy says it will be too noisy for me as I have delicate ears and suffer with ear aches a lot. I have an ear ache at the moment and have to have squirty drops put in my ears. It is horrible and I do not like it. Mummy Cathy and Daddy Kevin have bought Eleanor some moon sand and a moon sand food maker. I hope it does not make too much mess. You will be in trouble Mummy cathy!!!

My friend Eric has been back to see me. He seems to live near by now as mummy Cathy hears him snoring in the mornings when she is getting ready for work. I am glad he is okay.

Daddy Kevin has gone to pool again with no stick or towel. I have never gotten to the bottom of this. I have also never managed to meet Gym or find out who he is. He must be Daddy Kevins invisible friend.

I have managed to save a great many little white balls. I do try to warn them when they are going to be hunted. They must always be on their guard.

Today is mummy Cathy and daddy Kevin's wedding anniversary. They are both truly happy. The fashion it seems nowadays is to renew wedding vows. I do not understand this. It is supposed to be the most wonderful day of your lives when you marry the person whom you truly wish to spend the rest of your days with. Why would you need to repeat it. Mummy Cathy thinks the only reson she can think of is if someone has broken their vows at some point and feels the need to make a show that all is well when actually all they are doing is papering over the cracks. Look at how many celebs that renew later go on to divorce. Mummy Cathy and daddy Kevin may not be rich financially but as a happily married couple they are minted with joy, happiness, love and respect for each other. Happy Anniversary to my wonderful mummy Cathy and daddy Kevin. XXXXXXXXXXX I have been lazy lately. I have had mummy Cathy home with me as she has been poorly. She is much better now and looking forward to going back to work. This also means that I will be expected to work as well. I have had some time off to look after mummy Cathy. I am really good at this. When she has been sleeping I sneak on to the bed, just to check she is okay and I accidently drop off to sleep next to her. It is not my fault that the bed is sooo comfy is it? Daddy Kevin has gone to a bookies today. I think this must be like a library. Apparently they have newspapers and televisions in them. Daddy Kevin must go there to watch the news in peace. Funny thing is though, sometimes he comes home with money that he didn't have before he went there. Daddy Kevin says he wins it. He writes things down about football games and comes home with bits of paper which he takes back and they give him money. I am not sure how this works. Mummy Cathy doesn't go to the bookies. She has enough books to read at home. Daddy Kevin has also taken his big bag with him so I guess he is going to see Gym. He did ask me if I wanted to go swimming with him. Now this is really strange because if he is going to the pool where was his big stick? Mummy Cathy is cooking them a nice dinner this evening. This is good for me as I know they will share. I hope sooo anyway as I am starving!!! Mummy Cathy took some steak, and a large turkey breast out of the freezer. The turkey is for tomorrow but the steak is for later. Yummmmy, I cannot wait. Mummy Cathy never eats all of hers so I know she will share. I am resting now and building up my appetite. Eric has not been back since Mummy Cathy and my sis Michelle saw him last week. Maybe he has been sent to fat camp to work his tummy off. I am sure he will be back soon. Mummy Cathy is going into the food room (kitchen) now so I will have to follow her. Just to see if she needs my help with anything......

I was chatting with mummy Cathy and daddy Kevin about rabbits and rabbit warrens. Daddy Kevin says that rabbit holes that look like the hole is filled means the rabbits have moved to a different warren. Mummy Cathy says she has watched the wildlife documentary called water ship down. It had the rabbits called fiver and blackberry in. Sad at the end. Mummy Cathy cried. Anyway the point is when fiver and blackberry went in their holes they kicked the earth in with their back legs to close the door to keep out unwanted bunnies. So just because the warrens look empty, they are not. They are just sleeping and enjoying the privacy with their doors shut. David Attenborough didn't make water ship down. He was probably busy in a zoo making a programme about polar bears or something. I like rabbits. I have seen lots this weekend while i have been walking with daddy Kevin. You should see how fast they run. Whoosh, all you see are their little cotton tails. David Attenborough would never keep up with them now he is getting on in years. I is shattered.

Hello peeps, I haven't been on f/b in a while. Mummy Cathy has been poorly. Mummy Cathy has always suffered with migraines but lately it is different. Mummy Cathy has been to the doctor's who have not diagnosed the problem yet. She was given some pills but can only take 1 a day. Mummy Cathy takes this first thing in the morning when her head is exploding. The pill helps for a while but then by lunchtime her head is starting to throb again. She has to go back to the doctors again on Monday and is being referred to a neurologist. Obviously being a worrier and because of the questions the doctor asked she is thinking the worst. Poor mummy Cathy!!! Mummy Cathy has told me to shut up and chat about happy things. Well we went to Dawlish Warren 2 weeks ago. OMG, it was such fun. Mummy Cathy and Daddy Kevin walked me for miles across something called the Dunes. We walked about 7 miles. Ohhhh my poor legs, they was dropping off!!! Mummy Cathy and daddy Kevin went blackberry picking. I don't know why? Don't they sell them in Tesco? Mummy cathy had scratches all down her legs but still she laughed. The funniest thing was though. Sorry mummy Cathy. Daddy Kevin took me down a steep sand bank onto the beach. It was quite steep. Mummy Cathy is afraid of heights (and most other things) and so couldn't run down it like us. We were not expecting what she did next. She sat down and shuffled down on her bottom. You should have seen her bottom and legs, all covered in damp sand. Daddy Kevin said, "you are not getting in the car looking like that". Daddy Kevin didn't mean it though. We stayed in a chalet and it was really nice. I had my own bedroom which even had a quilt on it. I didn't sleep on it though, I just used it to wipe my mouth after my dinners. If I had done this at home I would have been told off!!! Bedtimes were the best as I thought I would be able to sleep with mummy Cathy and daddy Kevin. I managed to sneak in between them a couple of times and daddy Kevin didn't even moan at me. Mind you he had drank a couple of pints before bedtime. I also made a mistake a couple of times and got on the bed before daddy Kevin had gotten in. He was not happy with this. He wanted to know where he was meant to sleep. I did offer him my bedroom. Oh I almost forgot to tell you about all of the rabbits and hares we saw when we were on our midnight pee pee walks. Hundred's of them. They ran so fast all we got to see were there little white bob tails. Mummy Cathy said we saw more hares than daddy Kevin has on his head. Sorry daddy Kevin. Daddy Kevin was so pleased with me on this little holiday. He had bought me a knew lead and collar. It is called the figure 8 lead and is designed to stop me pulling and jumping up. I have been a god boy because it worked and I was well behaved. It might have been just because I was exhausted from walking though!!! When we got home I was so tired I slept for almost a week solid. Daddy Kevin wants to go back there as both daddy Kevin and mummy Cathy loved it there so much. I think they are just trying to shrink me down. It is nice to walk in the cooler weather because in the hot weather I struggle to breathe and cannot walk far. Anyway for now I am shattered just from thinking about that weekend. I shall dream about the bunnies......red now and going to grab 40 winks before I have my tea........

In all of my excitement last week when I was telling my story I forgot to tell you about my brother Michael. He came round to visit mummy Cathy. Mummy Cathy cooked his tea. They had a mid week roast. Michael's favourite. It was pouring with rain while he was at our house and he had to pop back to his friend Holly's house. Michael has been friends with Holly since they were teenagers and he is a god parent to her 2 girls. Michael rode off on his bike to Holly's and back within 10 minutes. When he walked back through the door he was saturated. Mummy Cathy sent Michael upstairs to dry his hair. Mummy Cathy told Mike to take his socks and jeans of and put into the tumble drier. He gave a shy look, and mummy Cathy laughed and said, I have seen you walking around in your boxers shorts many times before. Mummy Cathy has been feeling so poorly she was happy to see Michael and chat with him. I was not so happy with him having dinner at ours as Michael NEVER shares with me. Greedy Pig. Oh I was wrong. He shared a little piece of meat with me. Sorry Mike you are not such a greedy pig after all.

I am not happy. Daddy Kevin should have been home by now but has had to work overtime. This means that when he gets home both daddy Kevin and mummy Cathy will be going straight out again as mummy Cathy has to go back to the doctors. I will not get the chance to look in daddy Kevin's bag to check it out for food. Daddy Kevin sometimes brings me a sarnie home. Not often mind you.

Mummy Cathy has made pumpkin soup and rice pudding today for tea. I am not sure what pumpkin soup is but I like rice pudding. Yummy!!!

It must be nap time now while I wait for daddy Kevin to come home......

Daddy Kevin and y brother Michael have been rescuing animals today. I have told mummy Cathy that I do not want to share my beds with other animals as the last time they were thinking of rescuing another dog (remember Tyson) it didn't go at all well for me. Tyson attacked me and I still have the scars to show from it. Mummy Cathy has told me, they are just playing a game called Pet Rescue. I am not happy at this, pets need a happy home and it shouldn't be treated as a game. Am I missing something? Apparently it isn't real. It is just a game on phones and tablets to win points and not real animals being saved. I am a bit happier now. For a minute there I thought daddy Kevin was going to trade me in for another, better behaved dog.

I was a little bit naughty earlier. I stole a pair of daddy Kevin's socks from the bedroom. I was so pleased with myself. I sneaked into the bedroom, sneaked out. I ran down the stairs and into the garden. Mummy Cathy was reading the paper and didn't even look up as I slid across the kitchen floor to escape with my goodies. I was good in the end though as I did give the socks back and in return was given a sausage from the fridge. Who says crime doesn't pay. Haha.

Daddy Kevin has taken Michael to play football now. Michael plays 5 a side football on a Sunday evening somewhere out in the countryside. when Michael lived at home with us, he always used to come home with a bright red face and grazed knees from falling over.

There have been lots of fireworks going off for the last few days. They do not bother me though. I am lucky as I am getting older my hearing isn't what it was. Unless mummy Cathy shouts dinner is ready. I always hear this.

I saw my nanny Brenda and grampy Dennis yesterday. They came to see me. It is nearly my birthday. It is also nanny Brenda's birthday and my cousin Olivia's. Olivia will be 7 like me. I cannot count as far as nanny Brenda's age though. Sorry nanny Brenda.

Mummy Cathy has just cooked daddy Kevin 2 corn on the cobs. Daddy Kevin gets all messy while he eats these. Butter drips all down his face. Daddy Kevin has also had a big roast dinner today. There was nothing left for me today as my piggy brother Michael came for lunch and scoffed it all. Michael does enjoy mummy Cathy's dinners. Message to Michael, so do I.

I am going to end now as Daddy Kevin is having his tea and he may just drop some on the floor for me to find. Hopefully.......

What a strange day I had yesterday. Daddy Kevin had promised to take me and mummy Cathy to the woods where he used to ride his mountain bike and go running. Mummy Cathy was worried in case the paths were really muddy or slippy. Daddy Kevin assured us the paths were safe. Daddy Kevin said the paths were old stony paths and comfortable for walking on.

Mummy Cathy cooked bacon sandwiches before we left so that we wouldn't be hungry. Both mummy Cathy and daddy Kevin shared with me. Mummy Cathy then started to tell me scary stories about the woods. Mummy Cathy told me to be careful of the 3 bears as they might think I am goldilocks with my white fur. Then she told me about the big bad wolf. As I have a red coat mummy Cathy said the wolf might think I was little red riding hood. By now I am petrified. I am going to be gobbled up by either 3 bears or a wolf.

Anyway off we set in the car. It was along way to go. It took over half an hour to get to the woods. It s next to where daddy Kevin went to high school. It was nearly by where nanny Brenda and grampy Dennis lives. Daddy Kevin parked the car and off we went. It was up hill and mummy Cathy was already moaning. Mummy Cathy doesn't really like the countryside. We had only been walking a couple of minutes and there covered in mud was a teddy bear. I sniffed it and remembered mummy Cathy's story about the 3 bears. I was beginning to worry. We carried on walking and I looked at the trees and sniffed all of the strange smells. I was having a lovely time. Mummy Cathy had stopped moaning and seemed to be enjoying the walk also. We carried along the path for a couple of miles. We passed the first bath back and carried on to the next. Daddy Kevin said the view from the top was fabulous. Off we walked again. Me sniffing and peeing on every other tree, marking my way back in case we got lost. We then came to a steep grassy7 muddy path. Daddy Kevin decided we had walked far enough and it was time to go back to the car. We never got to the see view. Disappointing. Anyway here comes the best bit and pay back for mummy Cathy trying to scare me about the woods. The path was very muddy and very slippy. Mummy Cathy was taking baby steps so as to stay upright. Daddy Kevin was telling mummy Cathy where to walk and be safe. The next thing mummy Cathy screamed and she was on her backside. Daddy Kevin came to her all concerned. I tried to jump on her as I thought she was sat down having a rest. Daddy Kevin helped mummy Cathy up. Mummy Cathy was covered in mud. Her legs, her coat and her trousers. Mummy Cathy was cursing all of the cyclists who ride up and down the path, tearing up the grass and making it muddy. Mummy Cathy says they are vandals and should be banned from riding through the forests. We made our way gingerly back to the car and mummy Cathy took her coat of and socks and boots. Thankfully she had taken her old slippers with her as we were visiting nanny Brenda and grampy Dennis on the way home. Grampy Dennis is on the mend now thankfully from prostrate cancer. We are all really happy about this. By the time I had finished running up and down their garden I was shattered when we got home. That was me asleep for the night. As for the bog bad wolf and the 3 bears we didn't see them. I didn't have nightmares last night I just laughed in my sleep at mummy Cathy on all fours covered in mud. Me and daddy Kevin will be laughing about this for weeks. Sorry mummy Cathy but it was funny...

Well I think this is the end for now before I get into trouble. I will keep on writing and telling people what I am getting up to. I hope you all enjoy my tales and have a giggle. As for mummy Cathy she is a lovely selfless mummy and I love her and daddy Kevin with all my heart. I am getting old now as I am 49 (7). My hearing is starting to go and I am getting slower in my movements. I am a very spoilt dog and am lucky to want for nothing. I am truly living The Life of Riley. XXXXXX

I is sorry for all the repititions and typo error's.
Remember I is only a pup.

2007/04/13 23:57

2007/03/09 22:37

2007/05/27 21:49

MUDDLE

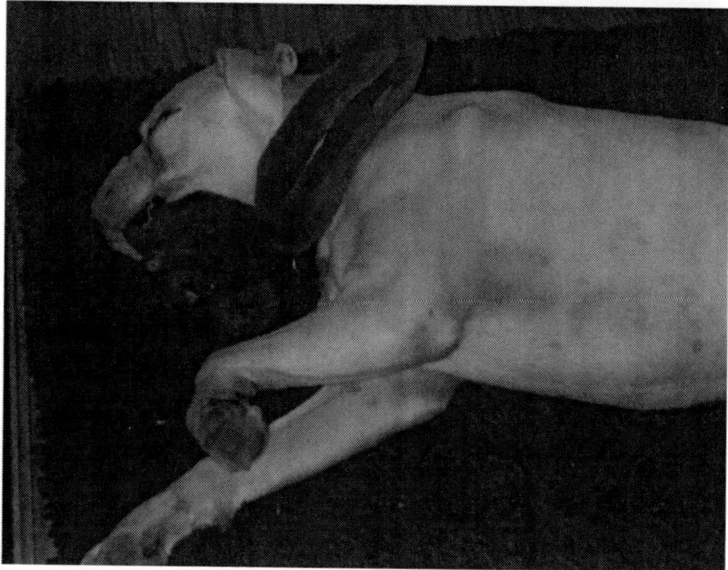

2007/05/30 17:17

2007/05/14 21:57

2007/06/01 19:39

2007/05/19 17:21

2007/06/01 19:36

2007/03/13 20:02

2007/03/27 21:17

2007/04/13 23:57

2007/04/08 09:25

2007/03/29 22:11

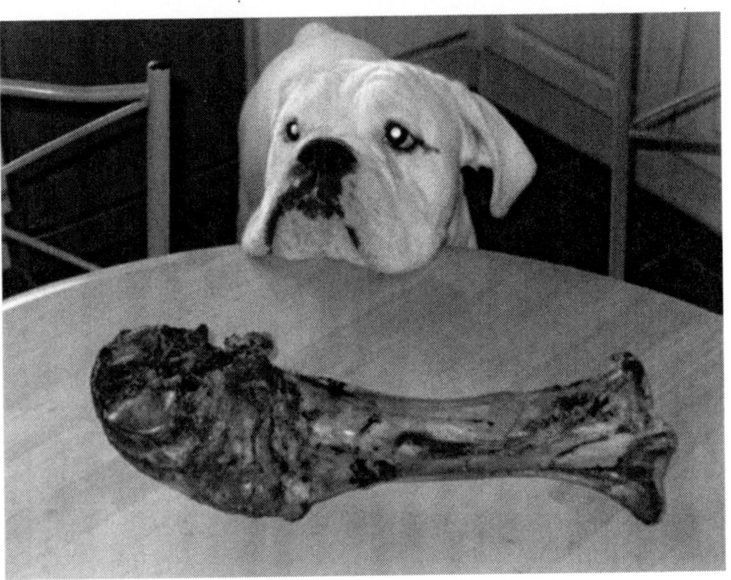

CHEWERS

2007/03/04 00:43

2007/04/13 23:57

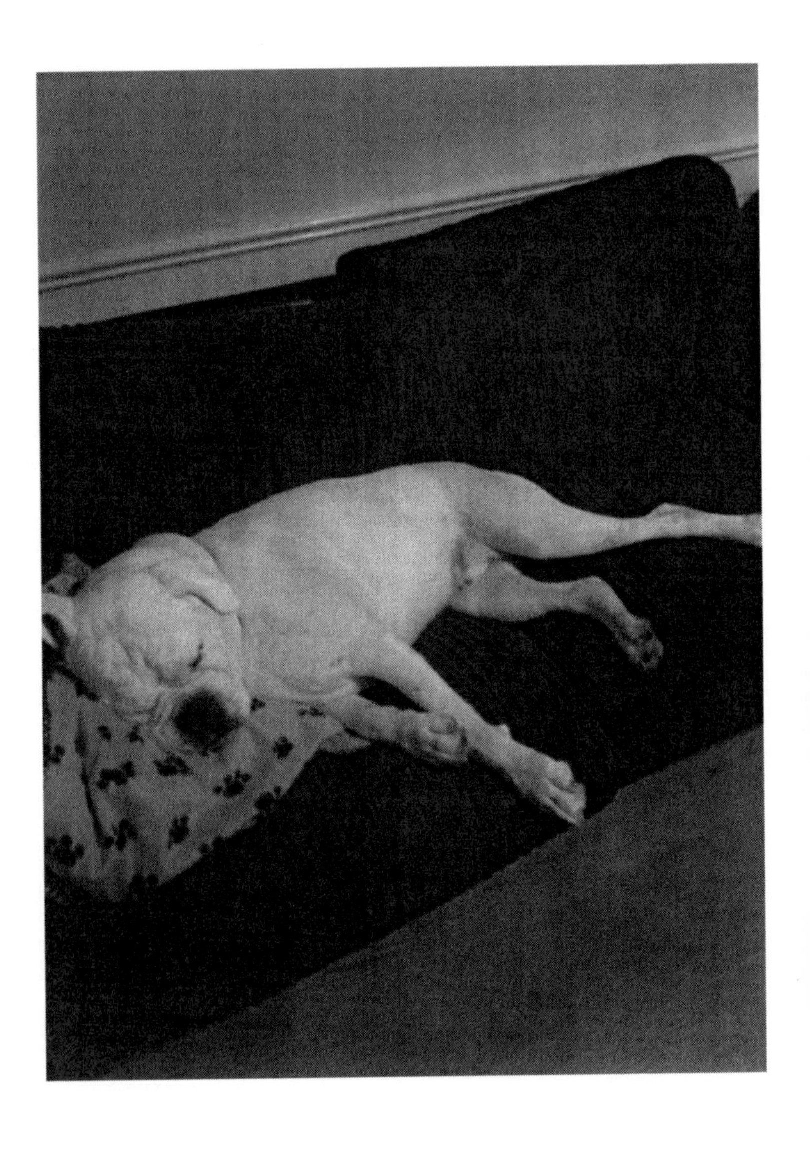

2007/03/10 00:52

2007/04/13 23:57

03/29 22:09

Lightning Source UK Ltd.
Milton Keynes UK
UKOW03f0255140514

231645UK00001B/7/P